D1403974

SIMPLE & DELICIOUS
JAPANESE COOKING

SIMPLE & DELICIOUS
JAPANESE
COOKING

Keiko Hayashi

Tokyo • **Shufunotomo/Weatherhill** • New York

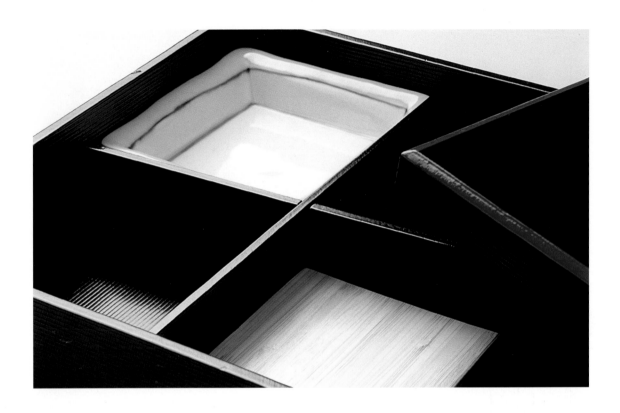

First Printing, 1999

All rights reserved throughout the world.
No part of this book may be reproduced in any
form without permission in writing from
the publisher.

© Copyright in Japan 1999 by Keiko Hayashi
Photographs by Yoji Yamada
English text supervised by Jane Singer
Editor: Michiko Kinoshita
Assisted by Hiro Tega
Stylist: Reiko Takeyama
Book design by Office 21
Jacket design by Liz Trovato

Published jointly by Weatherhill, Inc.
41 Monroe Turnpike, Trumbull, CT 06611, U.S.A.
and Shufunotomo Co., Ltd.
2-9, Kanda Surugadai, Chiyoda-ku, Tokyo 101-8911, Japan

ISBN 0-8348-0425-5

Printed in China

INTRODUCTION

Like many people, I learned my most important lessons in life at home. From the age of four, I began to receive basic cooking instructions at home, and since then, I have honed my cooking skills and created new recipes in my own kitchen. That is where I polish my culinary techniques, experiment with new dishes, and nurture new ideas for my cooking.

My paternal grandmother was my first cooking teacher. As was the custom in Japan, she lived with the family of her eldest son, my father. Her approach to preparing meals was sincere and heartfelt, influenced in no small measure by her father-in-law, who was a master of the tea ceremony. Dishes served in the tea ceremony are prepared with the utmost concern, with care being taken to ensure that they reflect seasonality, avoid duplication of ingredients and cooking techniques, and prove pleasing, in both taste and presentation, to the invited guests.

My mother had to satisfy the refined tastes of a husband raised in such a family. I can remember that she spent much time everyday in the nearby market carefully selecting the ingredients for our dinner. She also benefitted from a basic training in Western, Chinese and Japanese cooking in her courses at bridal school, which were requisites for young women at that time who were preparing for marriage.

With this family background, it is not surprising that I have always paid a little extra attention to what we eat at home. So has my husband. But our schedules and demands have always been far different from those in my mother's or grandmother's time. Although I have always tried to prepare the special celebratory dishes that are traditional for the New Year, seasonal dishes based on the Japanese calendar, and popular family treats, I have been restricted by the need throughout our married life to save time and money. Cooking time was limited because I worked part-time, but I strongly resisted sacrificing the quality of our meals at home. This presented a tremendous challenge to me each day.

My efforts in this area eventually bore fruit, and I began to share my experiences at home with others, through local publications and other mass media. Then I took the next step and began teaching classes for foreign residents in Tokyo, who, I found, faced much of the same challenge in their lives in Japan.

In the meantime, I read hundreds of cookbooks and culinary works which my husband thoughtfully bought for me, both at home and abroad, and I began writing my recipes in English. I rewrote them many times, reflecting the questions that arose in my cooking classes, and I tested them with my students in each class. Shufunotomo Co., Ltd. first published my collected recipes in 1969, and that book is now in its seventh printing.

The popularity of my recipes has been summarized in this way:

The recipes are easy to follow at home, and I try to anticipate any questions you may have.

If you follow the directions, you can produce dishes that are exactly as you have pictured them beforehand.

All of the photographs featured in this book were taken at my home. I myself prepared every dish that is shown in my own kitchen, with the others involved in the book double-checking the taste and presentation. What I found most encouraging was the fact that the other staff members brought home all the leftovers after they had tasted them. The dishes that I have introduced in the book clearly represent foods that are very popular among Japanese today when they cook at home.

I am thankful that with this book, I could at last respond affirmatively to friends who have urged that I write a sequel to my first work. I hope you enjoy *Simple & Delicious Japanese Cooking*.

Keiko Hayashi

CONTENTS

MEASUREMENTS AND EQUIVALENTS

Spoons & Cups	Metric	American	Metric
1 teaspoon	5 cc	$1/6$ oz.	5 g
1 tablespoon	15 cc	$1/2$ oz.	15 g
2 tablespoons	28 cc	1 oz.	28 g
1 cup	230 cc	8 oz.	230 g
(16 tablespoons)			
2 cups (1 pint)	450 cc	1 lb.	450 g
		(16 oz.)	
4 cups (1 quart)	900 cc	2 lbs.	900 g

Japanese Cuisine: Reflecting Nature's Bounty

"The Land of Ripening Ears of Rice" was the appellation Japanese bestowed on their land in olden days. Even today, if you travel throughout the country in the early autumn, in every direction you will see fields of golden rice stalks, bowing in the breeze. It is plain to see that rice has always been the staple food of Japan.

Rice alone, of course, does not a meal make. Japan is surrounded by the sea; the country itself consists of over 3,000 islands, although most Japanese live on the four main islands. The country's southwestern shores are washed by warm water from the Southern Pacific, while the chilly Northern Pacific currents reach the northern coasts. These warm and cold currents meet not far from Tokyo, creating a fertile environment for a variety of fish. Thus seafood has always been an important source of protein. In addition to the fish and other seafood caught along the long coastlines, Japanese have long savored the fish from northern and southern seas that are harvested nearby.

The country is also known for its hilly, often mountainous terrain. Hills and mountains cover 70% of Japan's land area, and much of this is forested land, from which Japanese harvest nuts, yams, mushrooms, edible plants and other forest crops. On the remaining flat space and the terraces carved into the hillsides are rice paddies and fertile fields where rice and vegetables are grown.

On the main island of Honshu, where the great majority of the Japanese live, each of the four seasons has its own distinct character, and Japanese greatly appreciate the taste of seafood and vegetables harvested in season. Seasonality is one of the most important factors in Japanese cooking, as with much of Japanese culture. In one of his books, restaurateur Kaichi Tsuji, of the famous *kaiseki* restaurant Tsujitome in Kyoto, writes that at one time "I only used vegetables grown within 10 *ri* (about 2.5 miles) of my home and during the ten days or so when they were at their peak." This 10-day period when food is at its best in season is called *shun* in Japanese. Food that is in season (*shun*) is not only tastiest, but it is also economical, because it is usually available in abundance.

Thanks to this bounty of land and sea, most Japanese are able to enjoy a great variety of fresh foods throughout the year.

The Tastes and Flavor of Japan

Every country has its own distinctive tastes and flavors. In Japanese cooking, these can be best characterized by the ingredients that go into making Japanese soup stock and the seasoning agents, herbs and spices most often used to flavor Japanese foods.

Due to the country's lack of extensive pasture lands and the local prohibition, in force for centuries, on eating meat, Japanese farmers never developed meat or dairy products. Animal fats were also uncommon until Chinese and Western cooking were introduced in the mid-19th century. Instead, grains became an important part of the Japanese diet.

Soy beans, together with other grains, are the major ingredients in soy sauce (*shoyu*) and soybean paste (*miso*). Japan's wet climate and natural humidity helped encourage the development of fermentation technology, essential for producing such local delicacies as pickled vegetables, *shoyu* and *miso*.

Japanese also learned how to use their native seafood, sea plants and mushrooms to best effect, by themselves or to complement other foods. A particular species of sardines, for example, is dried to preserve it and used in a soup stock. Fillets of bonito fish are steamed, smoked, dried and flaked, then used as a basic ingredient for making soup stock. Kelp is dried and also used for stock, to impart a totally different flavor to the soup. Dried kelp and dried *shiitake* mushrooms play an equally important role in soup-stock production in Japanese vegetarian cooking.

Japanese corporate scientists have worked hard to identify the essential ingredients behind the tastes of favorite local dishes, and today you can purchase prepared, bottled flavoring agents of all kinds at supermarkets in Japan. However, in general, herbs and spices are not used as much in

Japanese cooking as in the West. Since Japanese try to savor the natural taste and flavors of the food itself, any flavoring additives, including herbs and spices, are kept to a minimum. They are intended to enhance the food's own taste, rather than to be appreciated on their own. Therefore, herbs and spices used in Japanese cooking tend to be mild in flavor, and they are added in small quantities. Japanese cooks take care not to obscure the natural tastes of the foods they are cooking. Harmony of flavors and ingredients is extremely important.

Fresh, mild-tasting natural herbs are often used to indicate the season in Japanese cooking. Other herbs and spices, like ginger, are used to counter the possibly unpleasant odors of such foods as fish. Still others, such as Japanese horseradish (*wasabi*) and ginger, are intended to destroy bacteria that may be contained in raw foods like *sashimi*, to reduce the risk of food poisoning.

A wide variety of citrus fruits are grown in the warm western parts of Japan. Their juice is often added to other foods for a mildly bitter and piquant taste. They impart their individual flavor, unique to each citrus variety, while they help announce the arrival of their season.

The Japanese Melting Pot

My husband and I once took a friend from China, who was visiting Tokyo, to a casual Chinese restaurant for lunch. When we asked her impressions of the Chinese food she had just eaten, she asked, with a note of surprise, "Is this Chinese?"

When I ask the members of my cooking classes for Westerners what dishes they want to learn to cook, many of them mention foods that, to Japanese, appear to be Western, such as fried chicken or pork cutlets. Yet these are Japanese-style dishes, cooked differently from their Western equivalents, and prepared with a distinctively Japanese flavor.

Japan has welcomed many new foods and cooking techniques from abroad throughout its history. Most of them have been adapted to suit local tastes over the years. Many are now undergoing changes to adapt them to the Japanese palate. Japan has become a culinary melting pot.

In prehistoric times, rice was first brought to Japan from continental China. The rice that Japanese commonly eat today is a slightly sticky, short-grain rice called japonica, unlike the indica strain typically eaten by the Chinese people.

Buddhism was first introduced to Japan more than 1,000 years ago by monks from China and Korea. They brought not only their religion and civilization, but their dietary habits and favorite foods. They discouraged the killing of animals and promoted a national ban on eating meat, which officially lasted until the mid-19th century.

Many young Japanese monks were sent to China for Buddhist study over the centuries that followed. They returned home to introduce the dishes they had enjoyed in China and cooking ingredients and techniques which were new to the Japanese. Chinese influences on Japanese cuisine at that time were mainly confined to such vegetarian foods as the tofu dishes often cooked by Zen Buddhists. These foods have also been modified locally over the years.

Western influences on the Japanese diet were first felt with the initial visits of Portuguese and Spanish merchants in the mid-16th century. With Japan officially closed to the rest of the world for more than 250 years during the Edo period (1600–1868), foreign traders were only allowed access to Nagasaki, on the Southern island of Kyushu, but through this narrow conduit, they introduced European and Chinese dishes that had a continuing impact on Japanese cuisine. Tempura is one of the imported dishes that dates from this time.

More extensive Westernization of Japanese cuisine began after the Meiji Restoration in 1868. From then on, Japanese were officially allowed to eat beef and pork, dishes that had formerly been reserved to the elite as "medicinal food." A great variety of Western and Chinese dishes were actively introduced to the Japanese, with their tastes modified to suit the native palate. Most were first introduced in restaurants, but gradually became common dishes in the home.

In the half-century since the end of World War II, Japanese have developed an ever-increasing fondness for foreign dishes, especially those originating in China and the West.

Appreciating Food with All Our Senses

We eat with our mouths, but we appreciate food with more than just our taste buds. Japanese, especially—both those who prepare the food and those who eat it—are taught to appreciate their food with all their senses.

We first savor food with our eyes. The arrangement of food on a dish or in a bowl and the presentation of the dishes on the table should favorably impress those sitting at the table and help to stimulate their appetites. There are no strict rules in arranging food on a plate or presenting it at the table, but like a painter with his palette, good chefs will pay strict attention to the combination of colors that are presented. The shape and size of the food is also important: Not only should the food on the plate look attractive and mouth-watering, it should also be cut and prepared so that guests can easily retrieve it with chopsticks and place it in their mouths. If suitable care is taken in visual preparation, the guest will appreciate, at a glance, the cook's thoughtfulness and the warm welcome that is expressed in the food before him or her.

Before you touch the food on your plate, you will make all kinds of assumptions and impressions based on its aroma alone. The subtle aroma of the food may impart specific memories or sensations, as does the rich fragrance of *matsutake* mushrooms in autumn. With one's nose, you can detect a flavor that is nearly hidden, but which the host secretly hopes that you will recognize and enjoy. In daily life, the appeal to the nose is often more pronounced. Many Japanese, for example, experience a feeling of nostalgia for their childhoods when they broil a slice of saury mackerel in the late summer. In vegetarian cooking, however, cooks take care not to overstimulate our olfactory organs, abstaining from much use of garlic or onions in their dishes.

One's nose also plays an important role in identifying whether the food being served is something that you like, dislike, or have not yet tasted. If you remember the smell, you may be subtly reminded of a pleasant or unpleasant experience related to eating the food. Without assistance from your sense of smell, you would be unable to appreciate the real flavor and taste of the food.

Once you have picked the food up from your plate, you will begin to appreciate it with your tongue, as you enjoy the unique texture of each food. As the many Japanese expressions about the feel of the food in one's mouth indicate, you can appreciate food from the sensations imparted as you chew it, whether it is chewy *konnyaku* (devil's tongue), silky tofu or crunchy abalone. You will also enjoy the smooth sensation of swallowing fine noodles, like angel-hair pasta floating in a broth.

The aural, or hearing, sense can also help you enjoy your food. The satisfying crunch of such foods as pickled radish, preserved herring roe or rice crackers, makes eating more pleasurable, and for Japanese, slurping with gusto as you swallow noodles from hot broth is considered a heartfelt gesture of appreciation of the food. Sipping hot tea while loudly sucking in cooling air is also permissible, so you can feel free to enjoy these hot dishes with plenty of sound effects.

The most important considerations in Japanese cooking are the ingredients of a dish and the way they are to be combined. Selecting food ingredients depends on the season, the guests' preferences, repetition and other factors. Orchestrating suitable ingredients for the occasion, the guest of honor and other guests, while expressing seasonality, is key. Harmony and balance are especially important. As in a vocal chorus, no single ingredient or flavor should stand out. Every ingredient used in cooking should find its most natural and appropriate place in the course of the meal. Just as we select our clothing to complement our appearance, we should carefully choose dishes and bowls that best complement the food we are to serve.

We prepare and present food with basically the same spirit as that of the host or hostess who prepares a *kaiseki* course for guests at a tea ceremony. This implies a desire to entertain the guest with thoughtfulness and sincerity.

Even at home, I try as much as possible to retain the original properties of the food I cook, to select cooking techniques that suit the tastes of those who will be eating it, to add a minimal amount of flavorings during cooking, and to produce a well-balanced meal which pleases all the senses.

Dining at Home

In my childhood days, which were not all so long ago, eating out was uncommon for Japanese. Either the mother or the grandmother prepared the family meals at home everyday. Traditionally, every meal featured plain white rice, either hot or cold. Fish, meat and/or vegetable dishes were prepared to go with the rice.

The rice was almost always served plain, without flavoring or seasonings of any kind, but there were a few exceptions. When fresh mushrooms, peas, bamboo shoots or other seasonal delicacies were available, they were cooked with the rice and the rice was lightly seasoned. On festive occasions such as birthdays or graduation days, the rice was cooked with red beans (*adzuki*) to dye the rice red, the color of celebration. At such times, a slightly sticky rice was used, and it was cooked with more than the usual amount of water, to ensure that the rice would be soft.

A variety of foods were served with rice. Since rice—bland but filling—was the meal's main dish, cooks often chose accompaniments that were salty, like salted, dried fish, or vegetables that were pickled using a natural fermentation process. A simple meal typically combined rice with some salty, preserved foods that were readily prepared.

A typical breakfast at home included rice, miso soup and pickled vegetables. Other popular foods at the breakfast table were raw eggs (beaten with a little soy sauce and mixed with the rice), laver (*nori*), fermented soybeans (*natto*) and lightly grilled dried fish. For lunch, most people who ate outside the home brought their own box lunch, or *obento*, consisting mainly of rice, a small piece of fish, pickled vegetables, and other common foods. Those who remained at home mainly dined on rice and the leftovers from the previous evening's meal.

Dinner was the biggest meal of the day, when the greatest variety of fish, meat and vegetable dishes were served. On a frosty winter evening, the family would sit around a bubbling pot containing seasonal fish and vegetables, which was placed on a table-top stove. The family would serve themselves directly from the pot as it cooked.

Internationalization of Japanese home cooking began with an increase in eating out. The always convenient curry and rice, for example, which most Japanese cook using a dried, prepared curry roux, first appeared at family-oriented restaurants in department stores. Today it is one of the most popular dishes among children. School lunches also helped to change dietary habits, by introducing such child-pleasing, time-saving dishes as hamburgers and spaghetti.

Cooking programs on television also contributed to expanding the variety of foods typically eaten at home. While Japanese are increasingly dining out and trying dishes that are new to them, they have also become more adventurous at home, and are trying their hands at all kinds of novel cuisines.

To reduce the kitchen workload and to satisfy these varying desires, Japanese are increasingly using instant and frozen foods. Most of these are Western or Chinese foods; traditional Japanese foods are commonly sold in small packs for immediate use, and may not be suitable for refrigeration.

Until recently, cooking classes were the domain of young girls, who wanted to learn Western and Chinese as well as basic Japanese cooking to prepare to be good wives. In recent years, cooking classes for men have also become popular. Today, many televised cooking programs target children, who want to prepare their own meals. These boys and girls, as they grow, will change our daily dietary habits even further.

Hors d'Oeuvres to Desserts

HORS D'OEUVRES

Sashimi **Platter**

(*Sashimi no Mori-awase*)

Sashimi is sliced raw fish or shellfish served with condiments, *wasabi* horseradish and shoyu.

Japanese love to eat fish, and they especially savor fish when served as *sashimi*. When eating any kind of raw fish, it is essential that the fish be very fresh. Most types of fish can be eaten raw only if they are quite fresh; that is, less than a day has passed since the fish was caught, even if it has later been frozen. However, there is one recognized exception: tuna and cuttlefish that are caught in the open sea and frozen on the spot aboard the fishing ship.

In the market, you can often purchase *sashimi* that has already been sliced and prepared. However, the *sashimi* will be more tasty if you purchase fresh fillets or blocks of fish for *sashimi* and slice them yourself at home.

4 servings
1 fresh squid (*ika*)
1 uncut sheet toasted *nori* laver
1 block tuna, 5 x 12 x 1.5 cm/2 x 5 x ½ inch deep
½ fillet (lower half) red snapper (*tai*), skinned
Condiments:
  10 cm/4 inch length *daikon*
    radish, peeled and finely
    shredded
  4 green *shiso* leaves
  4 stems *shiso* flowers (*ho-jiso*)
  1 tablespoon *beni-tade*
  1 knob *wasabi* horseradish,
    peeled and grated

1 Cut the squid lengthwise down the side to open it up. Hold onto the leg-like tentacles at the trunk of the squid and pull them off to remove the gut. Insert your fingers between the trunk and the triangular tentacle and pull the tentacle off—only the trunk will be used for *sashimi*. With a paper towel, pinch the outer skin of the trunk at its pointed end and pull the skin off, then rinse the skinned squid under running water and pat dry.

2 On a cutting board, score the skinned side of the squid lengthwise at 3 mm/⅛ inch intervals. Turn the squid upside down and place the sheet of *nori* laver atop it. Roll it up tightly from one end. Slice the roll into pieces 8 mm/⅓ inch thick. (Pictures 1–2)

3 Slice the block of tuna into bite-sized pieces. (Picture 3)

4 On a cutting board, place the red snapper fillet with the thicker end facing away from you and slice into pieces 8 mm/⅓ inches thick, holding the knife at a slight diagonal to the fish, with the back of the knife inclined towards you. (Picture 4)

5 Place the *daikon* radish in a mound covering one-third of the serving platter. Set the *shiso* leaves beside it. Arrange the prepared fish and squid next to the condiments. Prepare the other condiments and set alongside for serving.

6 Let each person place a teaspoonful of shoyu in an individual saucer and mix in a small amount of *wasabi* horseradish, then dip a slice of *sashimi* in the soy sauce before eating it. Alternatively, a small portion of *wasabi* may be placed directly on a slice of fish, which is dipped lightly in the shoyu, then eaten.

Marinated Horse Mackerel

(Aji no Kobu-jime)

This fish in vinegar marinade may be considered a variation of *sashimi*, because the fish is not cooked. It is not unlike such popular fish dishes as Scandinavian marinated fish and Mexico's ceviche. Be sure to get horse mackerel that is as fresh as the fish you would serve for *sashimi*.

8 servings
4 medium-sized fillets horse mackerel (*aji*)
1 tablespoon salt
4 tablespoons rice vinegar for rinsing the fish
3 pieces dried kelp (*dashi-kombu*), cut the length of the fish fillets
Marinade:
  2 tablespoons sugar
  ½ cup saké
  ½ cup rice vinegar
2 Japanese cucumbers, sliced paper-thin
  1 teaspoon salt
  1 tablespoon sugar
  1½ tablespoons rice vinegar
4 ginger flowers (*myoga*), shredded (optional)
4 green *shiso* leaves for garnish

1 Sprinkle both sides of the horse mackerel evenly with salt and let stand for a couple of hours or until the brine runs. Rinse salt from the fish by dipping quickly in rice vinegar and draining. Discard the vinegar.
2 Place 1 piece of dried kelp in a container large enough to hold all the fish fillets, and place 2 fillets on top of the kelp. Place another piece of kelp atop the fish, then lay down the remaining fillets. Top with the remaining piece of kelp.
3 Mix well the ingredients for the marinade and pour it over the fish. Marinate for 30 minutes. Discard the marinade and keep the fish and kelp in a refrigerator until serving, either immediately or the following day.
4 To serve, pinch the cellophane-like skin from near the head of the fish and pull it off along the fillet towards the tail.   (Picture above) Remove all the small bones you can see and slice the fillet into bite-sized portions.
5 Rub the cucumbers with salt and let stand for 5 minutes. Squeeze the brine from the cucumbers and mix in sugar and vinegar.
6 Dip shredded *myoga* in cold water for 1–2 minutes and drain well.
7 Arrange the horse mackerel, cucumbers, *myoga*, and *shiso* leaves on individual serving dishes before serving.

Spicy Squid

(Ika no Karami-ni)

4 servings
2 fresh squid (*ika*), gutted and skinned
2 dried red chili peppers, seeded and
  chopped (*taka no tsumé*)
3 tablespoons sugar
4 tablespoons saké
3 tablespoons shoyu
2 tablespoons mirin
1 tablespoon rice vinegar

1 Cut lengthwise along the side of each squid and open it up. Score diagonally the surface of the main part of the squid and cut it into 2.5 x 5 cm/1 x 2 inch lengths. Cut the tentacles into 5 cm/2 inch lengths.
2 In a shallow pan, bring the red chili peppers, sugar, saké, shoyu, mirin, and vinegar to a boil. Add the squids and boil for 1 minute. Remove the squids from the pan and boil the cooking sauce for 1 minute. Return the squid to the pan

(Picture above) and boil again for 1 minute. Repeat this procedure as necessary, until the cooking sauce is thick enough to coat the squid nicely.

Wine-Steamed Clams

(Hamaguri no Saka-mushi)

get them to spit out the sand before cooking.

If you find any unopened shells after cooking, that indicates the clams died earlier. Do not try to open or eat them.

4 servings
20 large sea clams (*hamaguri*)
4 tablespoons saké
5 sprigs *mitsuba* trefoil, parboiled and finely chopped
1 lemon, cut into 4 wedges

1 Place clams in a shallow pan and sprinkle with saké.
2 Cover the pan tightly and cook over high heat until all the clamshells have opened.
3 Break off and discard the empty half shells. Sprinkle the clams with *mitsuba* trefoil and serve promptly with lemon wedges.

Note:
If the clams are sandy, keep them in salt water (1 teaspoon salt to 1 cup of water) for 4–5 hours to

Grilled Oysters in a Spicy Vinegar Sauce

(Kaki no Iridashi)

4 servings
16 fresh shelled oysters, rinsed and drained
  2 tablespoons saké
  1 tablespoon shoyu
Spicy Vinegar Sauce:
  4 tablespoons grated *daikon* radish
  1 teaspoon Japanese chili pepper paste
  (*kanzuri*)
  2 tablespoons chopped leek
  Juice from 2 lemons
  1 tablespoon shoyu
  1½ tablespoons mirin
1 square of toasted *nori* laver, shredded

1 Marinate oysters in the saké and shoyu for 20 minutes, turning over occasionally.
2 Mix the ingredients for the spicy vinegar sauce.

3 Heat an ungreased, non-stick skillet until very hot and cook the oysters over high heat until they are round in shape, turning them over once.
4 Place the oysters in individual serving bowls, pour the sauce over them and top with toasted *nori* laver. Serve immediately.

Octopus and Cucumber Salad with Mustard Dressing

(Tako to Kyuri no Karashi-sumiso)

Tako means octopus in Japanese. Octopus is usually sold boiled in the market, but raw, uncooked octopus is sometimes available.

4 servings
2 Japanese cucumbers, thinly sliced
½ teaspoon salt
4 small pre-boiled octopus legs, cut into
 1.3 cm/½ inch lengths
Mustard Dressing:
 2 teaspoons Japanese dry hot mustard
 2 teaspoons boiling water
 4 tablespoons sweet *miso* paste or *saikyo-miso*
 1½ tablespoons sugar
 2 tablespoons Japanese rice vinegar
 1 tablespoon mirin

1 In a colander, place cucumbers, sprinkle with salt and rub until the salt disappears. Let stand for 10 minutes and squeeze out the brine.
2 In a mixing bowl, mix the cucumbers and octopus, and divide them in 4 serving dishes.
3 Mix mustard vigorously with boiling water in a small bowl, and place the bowl upside down on a dish. Let it stand for a few minutes.
4 In a Japanese grinding bowl, place the mustard, *miso* paste, and sugar and grind well until well-mixed. Add vinegar and mirin, grinding well after adding until mixture is smooth. Pour the dressing over the octopus and cucumbers before serving. Each person should toss his or her salad before eating.

Fried Eggplant with *Miso* Paste

(Nasu no Dengaku)

This recipe may not sound too tempting, but I have found that this is one traditional Japanese dish that most Westerners enjoy. Not only have I included this recipe in my classes for new arrivals in Tokyo, but I also demonstrated how to prepare this dish to groups of Americans when I visited several cities in the United States. Everyone who sampled it liked it.

4 servings
8 Japanese eggplants, or 2 American eggplants
⅓ cup vegetable oil
Bean Paste Spread:
 4 tablespoons white sesame seeds,
  toasted and ground, see page 23
 4 tablespoons sweet *miso* paste or *saikyo miso*
 2 tablespoons sugar
 3 tablespoons mirin
2 teaspoons toasted white sesame seeds

1 Cut off the stems and tops of the eggplants and cut lengthwise in half.
2 Heat 3 tablespoons oil in a frying pan and sauté eggplants on both sides until brown and soft. Arrange them skin side down on a platter. Repeat with remaining oil and eggplants.
3 Mix ground sesame seeds, sweet *miso* paste, sugar and mirin. Spread the bean paste spread on the eggplants and top with the sesame seeds.

• If large American eggplants are used, cut them crosswise into 1cm/½ inch thick slices and cook in the same way.

Boiled Soybeans

(Edamame no Shio-yude)

Fresh soybeans are sold either on the branch or picked and packed in the pod in plastic bags. Try to select firm, ripe but still green pods.

Edamame literally means "beans on branches" but the cut soybeans in the pod are also called *edamame*.

1 bundle fresh podded soybeans on branches
  or 1 package (4 cups) harvested fresh
  soybeans in the pod (*edamame*)
Water to boil beans
1 tablespoon salt

1 Remove the pods from the branches and rinse. Do not remove the beans from the pods before cooking.
2 Place the pods in a pot with water to cover and add salt. Cover the pan and bring to a boil.
3 Right before boiling, slide open the cover slightly so the water doesn't boil over. Reduce heat to medium low and boil for 25 minutes. Drain and serve.

Note: The boiled soybeans in the pod served at restaurants and drinking spots are green due to a chemical additive. Soybeans boiled at home as described above do not look as green as those served at restaurants but are much tastier.

Chicken Livers with Japanese Pepper

(Tori Reba no Sansho-ni)

Liver is a popular ingredient in *yakitori*, and it is almost always included when Japanese men order *yakitori* to go with their drinks. Many seem to believe that they can get extra strength from liver.

6 servings
450 g/1 lb chicken liver, water to cook liver
⅓ cup saké
½ teaspoon rice vinegar
3 tablespoons sugar
⅓ cup shoyu
1 teaspoon powdered Japanese pepper
  (*kona-sansho*), or 1 tablespoon fresh Japanese
  peppercorns (*mi-zansho*)
2 tablespoons mirin
10 young *kinomé* leaves

1 Clean the liver, discarding fat, blood and membrane, and cut into bite-sized pieces.
2 In a pan, place the liver, enough water just to cover the liver, the saké, rice vinegar, sugar, half the shoyu and ½ teaspoon pepper or all the peppercorns. Cover the pan and cook over low medium heat until most of the liquid is absorbed. Add the remaining shoyu and mirin. After cooking for 10 more minutes, sprinkle on the remaining pepper.
3 Garnish with *kinomé* leaves if available.

SOUP

Egg Flower Soup

(Kakitama-jiru)

Many Japanese, when they want to add one more small side dish to a dinner, serve this soup. Children love this soup and mothers are happy to see their children's enjoyment. The key to cooking this soup is to ensure that the soup is very clear and the eggs are soft.

4 servings
3 cups *dashi* stock, see page 129
1 teaspoon salt
1 teaspoon shoyu
1 tablespoon Japanese potato starch
  (*katakuri-ko*)
2 tablespoons cold water
2 eggs, beaten
6 sprigs *mitsuba* trefoil, cut into 2.5 cm/1 inch
  lengths

1 In a soup pan, bring the stock, salt and shoyu to a boil.
2 Mix the starch and cold water and quickly stir into the boiling soup. Continue to boil for ½ minute until the starch dissolves.
3 Reduce the heat to low. Pour eggs into the soup through a slotted ladle, trying to cover the surface of the soup. Top with the *mitsuba*. Turn off the heat when you have poured in all of the eggs and cover the pan for about a minute, until the eggs are cooked through, yet still soft. (Do not stir the soup when you pour in the eggs, or the soup will become cloudy.)

Toasting Sesame Seeds

The method for toasting sesame seeds varies slightly depending on the thickness of the pan that is used. Use an empty pan that is clean and dry.

A thick pan does not heat up immediately, making it difficult to judge whether sesame seeds are cooked if you begin toasting the seeds when the pan is cold. Warm up a thick pan before adding the sesame seeds. A thin pan heats quickly, so preheating is not necessary.

1 Place just enough sesame seeds in the pan to cover it in thinly (Picture 1). Cook over medium heat, shaking the pan frequently until some of the sesame seeds pop and darken in color. Raw, uncooked sesame seeds are typically flat in shape; once they are toasted they become rounder.
2 Place the toasted sesame seeds in a Japanese grinding bowl (*suribachi*) and grind with a pestle (*surikogi*), grinding briskly against the sides of the bowl until the seeds turn into a rough powder. (Picture 2).

Clear Soup with Shrimp and Ginger Flowers

(Ebi no Kuzu-uchi to Myoga no Osuimono)

4 servings
8 medium-sized shrimp, shelled and
  deveined, with tails left on
2 teaspoons saké
3 tablespoons Japanese potato starch
  (*katakuri-ko*)
Water for cooking shrimp
Pinch of salt
2 ginger flowers (*myoga*), thinly sliced
Clear Soup:
  3½ cups *dashi* stock, see page 129
  ⅔ teaspoon salt
  1 teaspoon shoyu

1 Sprinkle the shrimp with saké to improve its
aroma.
2 Dredge the shrimp thoroughly in potato
starch.
3 Place the shrimp in salted boiling water, and
cook for 1 minute, or until they rise to the top of

the pot. Remove the shrimp and place them
with the ginger flowers in 4 individual soup
bowls.
4 Bring the ingredients for the clear soup
ingredients to a boil and pour into each soup
bowl before serving.

Matsutake Soup in a Tea Pot

(Dobin-mushi)

A delicious way to enjoy *matsutake* mushroom soup is to cook individual servings in small pots which look just like small teapots, or *dobin*. These pots are actually designed expressly for this kind of soup. The soup contains many other ingredients as well, such as seasonal nuts and seafood. And all these ingredients cooperate to produce a perfect balance in the taste of the soup.

4 servings

3½ cups *dashi* stock, see page 129
1 tablespoon saké
1 teaspoon salt
½ teaspoon shoyu
12 gingko nuts
3 fillets of chicken, strings removed and cut into bite-sized pieces
4 shrimp, shelled and deveined with tails on
1 *matsutake* mushroom, sliced thinly and stem tip removed
4 sprigs *mitsuba* trefoil, cut into 3 cm/1 inch lengths
4 pieces maple-shaped *yuzu* citrus rind

1 Combine stock, saké, salt and shoyu in a pot and bring to a boil, so salt dissolves.
2 Crack gingko nuts individually with a garlic press, taking care so as not to crush the nut meat, and remove the shells. Place the shelled gingko nuts in a shallow pan and add cold water to cover. Cook over medium heat, stirring the nuts and pressing them lightly with a slotted ladle to remove the skin. Drain the nuts.
3 In individual pots* for *dobin mushi*, place gingko nuts, chicken meat, shrimp and mushroom slices, and fill with the soup. Set each pot on a burner, bring to a boil and cook 1 more minute. Top with trefoil and *yuzu* rind, cover the pots and serve immediately.

*About *dobin-mushi* pots
The specially designed pot for *dobin-mushi* looks just like a small teapot. However, on top of the lid of the pot, there is a small inverted saucer. When you "drink" the soup, you use the small saucer as a soup bowl. When you want to eat the soup ingredients, you just remove the lid and eat them with chopsticks.

Country-Style Pork and Vegetable Soup
(Ton-jiru)

The word "*Ton-jiru*" literally means Pork Soup. This soup is especially popular among blue-collar workers, who appreciate its hearty richness. With its broad variety of ingredients, including pork and different root vegetables, it offers substantial nutritional value as well as a complex good taste. This kind of soup tastes even better if prepared in copious quantities in a deep soup kettle. You can often find *ton-jiru* served at drive-in truck-stops and similar kinds of restaurants along the highway.

4–6 servings

½ block yam cake (*konnyaku*), cut into
  1 x 5 cm/½ x 2 inch lengths
Water for boiling *konnyaku*
½ small burdock (*gobo*)
2 tablespoons vegetable oil
150 g/9 oz thinly sliced pork, cut into
  bite-sized pieces
200 g/8 oz *daikon* radish, peeled and
  cut into 1 x 5 cm/½ x 2 inch lengths
⅓ carrot, peeled and cut into
  1 x 5 cm/½ x 2 inch lengths
2 Japanese taro potatoes (*sato-imo*),
  peeled, sliced and rinsed
6 cups Japanese stock from mixed
  fish flakes, see page 130
3 to 4 tablespoons *miso* paste (amount
  depends on saltiness)
½ leek, chopped

1 Boil the *konnyaku* in water for 1 minute. Discard the water and continue to cook while stirring until the dry *konnyaku* starts to make noise when you stir it. (Picture 1)
2 Scrape the skin of the burdock and cut crosswise slits all the way around the burdock stalk at ⅛ inch/3 mm intervals. Slice shavings off of the burdock with a knife, just as if you were using the knife to sharpen a pencil, and dip the burdock in cold water as you slice it. (Picture 2). Let the shavings stand until the dipping water changes color, then rinse out the shavings and drain them in a colander.
3 Heat the vegetable oil in a soup pan and stir-fry the pork, *konnyaku*, burdock, *daikon* radish, carrot and yam potatoes for just a few minutes. Add the *dashi* stock and bring it to a boil, while occasionally skimming off the residue. Cover the pan and cook over medium heat for 15 minutes or until the vegetables are soft.
4 Place the *miso* paste in a ladle and dissolve it in some stock from the pan (Picture 4). Stir it into the soup. Add the chopped leek and turn off the heat. Serve while hot.

Miso Soup with Sea Clams

(Asari no Miso-shiru)

Clams taste excellent by themselves, so they don't need a strong-flavored dashi-based soup; a piece of dried kelp (*dashi-kombu*) will provide enough flavor for the stock. Clams sometimes contain sand, especially when they are fresh from the ocean. To remove the sand, keep the clams in salted water (5% solution) for a few hours. If kept in a place that's dark and quiet like the seabed, the clams will relax and spit out the sand. For a reason that's not quite clear to me, my mother used to place an iron knife in the salt water as well. At any rate, most clams sold at the grocery store are washed clean and are nearly free of sand.

4 servings
3½ cups water
1 piece dried kelp for stock-making
   (*dashi-kombu*), 10 cm/4 inches in length
1½ cups small sea clams (*asari*) in the
   shell, well washed
3 tablespoons light-colored *miso* paste
1 teaspoon finely sliced fresh ginger root

1 Put the water in a pot, add the dried kelp, and let it soak for 10 minutes.
2 Heat the pot and remove the kelp right before the water begins to boil. Add the clams and cook until the shells open.
3 While cooking the clams, place the *miso* paste in a ladle and dissolve it in ½ cup of soup from the pot. Stir into the soup.
4 Serve immediately, topped with ginger root.

Sesame *Miso* Soup with Eggplants and Noodles

(Nasu to Somen no Uchikomi-jiru)

I learned to make this soup from my grandmother and nowadays, I often make it in the summer for my family. It's a tasty soup, easy to make and nutritionally well-balanced.

4 servings
2 Japanese eggplants
3 cups *dashi* stock, see page 129
1 piece thin-fried tofu (*aburage*), shredded
3 tablespoons *miso* paste
1 bunch (50 g/2 oz) dried Japanese
  vermicelli noodles (*somen*)
3 tablespoons white sesame seeds, toasted
  and ground, see page 23

1 After cutting off their stems, cut the eggplants lengthwise in half and slice into 3 mm/$^1/_8$ inch-thick pieces. Dip them in cold water as you slice them to prevent discoloration and to remove bitterness.
2 Cook the eggplants in the stock over medium heat for about 5 minutes or until almost done. Add the fried tofu and season with *miso* paste. Add the *somen* noodles and stir well to separate them. Stir in sesame seeds and turn off the heat immediately. Do not boil the soup after you add the *miso* paste, as it loses its flavor.

Miso Soup with Snow Peas

(Saya-endo no Miso-shiru)

In May and June, with the appearance of fresh, bright green young leaves, many Japanese wives are tempted to prepare *miso* soup with fresh, crispy snow peas for their families. I don't know why, but I have recently read that men in Japan like this particular soup. I think that this is probably because for many men, this soup triggers good memories of the soup which their mothers used to make.

In the old days, many women, like my mother and grandmother, picked the freshest peas from their vegetable garden early in the morning and prepared the soup with the peas before the family got together around the breakfast table. Here is my mother's and my recipe.

3½ cups *dashi* stock, see page 129
1 piece thin-fried tofu (*aburage*), shredded
50 g/2 oz fresh snow peas, cut into halves
  with strings removed
3 tablespoons light-colored *miso* paste

1 In a soup pan, place the stock, fried tofu shreds, and peas. Bring to a boil and cook until the peas are almost done. Do not overcook the peas; they should still be bright green and somewhat crispy.
2 Add the *miso* paste with a ladle, diluting it with the stock in the pan. Serve immediately.

SEAFOOD

Deep-Fried Seafood Tempura

(*Tempura*)

Tempura is the well-known dish of batter-dipped, deep-fried seafood and vegetables. It is not easy to reproduce at home the light, crispy tempura that you can find at a good tempura restaurant, but practice makes perfect. If you follow this recipe, in time you will be able to produce scrumptious, light-tasting tempura.

For the best tempura, always:
• Select only the freshest materials.
• Select oil specifically for *tempura* rather than salad oil.
• Cook with a thick-walled, deep iron pan that will keep oil at a stable temperature, even when the ingredients are added.
• Use cake flour (*hakuriki-ko*) for the batter and always add chilled water to the flour. Stir the batter just a few times lightly, not for too long.
• Maintain the oil temperature of 180°C/365°F for seafood, 160°C/330°F for vegetables. Test the oil temperature by dropping a small amount of batter into the heated oil.
• If the heat drops below 140°C/285°F, the batter will sink to the bottom of the pan. If it rises above 190°C/375°F, the batter will float close to the surface of the oil. At the optimal temperature of around 180°C/365°, the batter will stay at the middle level momentarily, then rise slowly to the surface.

Tempura Ingredients:
8 shrimp, shelled, deveined and slit down the back
4 pieces smelt (*kisu*), boned and opened
1 trunk of squid (*ika*), skinned and cut into
  8 pieces, see page 127
8 fresh *shiitake* mushrooms, stems trimmed off
8 slices sweet potatoes, each 8 mm/⅓ inch thick
8 Japanese green peppers (*shishito*), slit on
  the surface to prevent bursting in the oil
4 green *shiso* leaves

Seafood Batter:	Vegetable Batter:
1 egg	1 egg
1 cup ice-water	¾ cup ice-water
1 cup cake flour	1 cup cake flour

Note: If it is available, it is easy to use a flour designed solely for tempura use (*tempura-ko*), at the ratio of 1 cup of tempura flour to 1 cup of water.

Dipping Sauce (*tentsuyu*):
  ¼ cup mirin
  ¼ cup shoyu

1 cup *dashi* stock, see page 129
1 cup grated *daikon* radish (to add to dipping
  sauce), drained in a colander
Salt and lemon wedges for seafood if desired

1 Prepare ingredients for tempura and dipping sauce. Combine dipping sauce ingredients and bring to a boil.
2 Start heating the oil to the right temperature.
3 Make the batter. First stir ice-water with a beaten egg, then stir in sifted flour. Use the batter soon after stirring, or it will get heavy.
4 Dip each ingredient in the batter, then drop a few ingredients at a time into the oil to prevent the oil temperature from dropping.
5 Remove each piece when its surface turns a crisp, golden brown.
6 Drain the oil thoroughly from each piece and dry on a wire rack. Serve promptly on a plate lined with paper for absorbing excess oil.
7 Place the dipping sauce and 2 tablespoons grated *daikon* radish in individual serving bowls. Dip the tempura in the sauce and eat. You may also wish to flavor the seafood with salt and/or lemon instead of dipping it in the sauce.

Easy Vegetable Tempura
(*Shojin-age*)

4 servings
1 Japanese eggplant, quartered lengthwise
8 Japanese green peppers, slit to prevent
  bursting during deep-frying
4 spears green asparagus, with fibrous
  part removed, each cut in thirds
1 small bulb onion, cut crosswise into
  slices 6 mm/¼ inch thick, then pricked with
  toothpicks (see picture)
1 medium sweet potato, cut into slices
  6 mm/¼ inch thick
Batter:
  ½ cup tempura flour mix (*tempura-ko*)
  1½ cups ice-water
Dipping Sauce:
  1½ cups *dashi* stock, see page 129
  3 tablespoons shoyu
  3 tablespoons mirin
⅓ cup grated *daikon* radish

1 When all the vegetables are prepared, heat the oil in a wok or deep frying pan to 170°C/350°F.

2 Mix the batter ingredients roughly in a mixing bowl, using the thick ends of cooking chopsticks. The batter should be slightly lumpy, not mixed until smooth.

3 Dip each slice of vegetable in the batter, one by one, and drop in the hot oil. Just cook a few ingredients at a time. Fry until the surface is golden brown and crisp. Remove from the frying pan and drain off the oil.

4 Combine the ingredients for the dipping sauce in a saucepan and bring to a boil. Serve in individual serving bowls, and set the grated *daikon* radish in small bowls alongside. Serve the tempura while hot.

Japanese Vegetarian Wisdom (*Shojin Ryori*)

Shojin cooking is the name for a variety of Japanese cuisine which disdains the use of meat, poultry and eggs, fish or shellfish. The "sho" of *shojin* literally means "to concentrate," and the "jin" means "to go forward" or "to make progress." As these words imply, *shojin* cooking originated and was developed at Zen Buddhist monasteries, where meal preparation and consumption were an integral part of the monks' daily discipline.

The concept of *shojin* cooking, in addition to many of the recipes and ingredients commonly used in this diet, was introduced to Japan from China in the 13th century by Zen monks who had gone to China to study Buddhism.

One of the returnee monks subsequently devised guidelines for *shojin* cooking and a textbook for preparing *shojin*-style meals, to help train student monks performing kitchen duties.

As the years passed, the greengrocers and food retailers who supplied Buddhist temples with vegetables and other foodstuffs learned how to prepare shojin dishes. They began to sell the prepared foods, instead of just the ingredients, to the temples, for lay people who were served meals after temple gatherings.

Shojin dishes in modern daily life:

Many vegetable dishes and other dishes incorporating *shojin* ingredients are prepared by Japanese consumers today. Such *shojin* ingredients as tofu and related products are now available throughout Japan, but other foods such as *yuba*, dried sheets of tofu, are still considered regional specialties in areas where Zen Buddhism originally flourished, like Kyoto, Kamakura and Nikko.

Today, you can sample traditional *shojin* dishes at *shojin ryori* restaurants operated by some temples in Kyoto, Tokyo and other cities. There are also some independent restaurants that specialize in *shojin* dishes.

At home, when there has been a death in the family and food is ordered from a Japanese restaurant to serve guests at the wake, *shojin* dishes are typically prepared.

Although the word "*shojin*" has lost its religious connotation, it is still used to mean "temple food," i.e. dishes using *shojin* ingredients that are prepared in the *shojin* style. The word "*shojin*" does not necessarily refer to "vegetarian food," which may include Western-style vegetable dishes.

Characteristics:

The following are common to all *shojin ryori*:

1 No trace of meat, poultry and eggs, fish or shellfish is used. Even soup stocks are prepared using kelp and/or *shiitake* mushrooms.

2 Only vegetable oil is used, not animal fat or fish oil.

3 No strong-flavored spices or herbs are employed. At the gate of some Zen temples you can still find an old sign that reads, "No fish or garlic is allowed within."

4 The *shojin* ingredients supply all nutritional requirements. For example, protein comes from soybeans and soybean products, vitamins from fresh and dried vegetables, and minerals from sea vegetables.

5 Portions are modest in size, as are meals.

Ingredients:

Vegetables, as introduced in the Vegetable Section
Soybean Products
  Tofu; Fresh tofu: *kinugoshi-dofu, momen-dofu*
  Broiled tofu: *yaki-dofu*
  Fried tofu: *atsuage, ganmodoki*
  Thin-fried tofu: *aburage*
  Freeze-dried tofu: *koya-dofu, kori-dofu,*
   shimi-dofu
  Dried sheet: *yuba*
  Fermented soybeans: *natto*
Wheat Flour Products
  Fu: *fu, nama-fu*
Potato Products
  Konnyaku
Dried Vegetables
  Dried *shiitake* mushrooms (*hoshi-shiitake*)
  Dried shredded radish (*kiriboshi-daikon*)
  Dried taro stems (*zuiki*)
  Dried gourd strips (*kampyo*)
Sea Vegetables
  Kelp, *Wakamé, Hijiki, Aramé, Nori*
Wild Plants
  Ferns, fiddlehead ferns, horsehead ferns

Steamed Fish with Ginger and Green Onions

(Sugata-mushi)

In Japanese cooking, fish are typically cut up for individual servings or sliced into bite-sized pieces. A single serving may consist of an entire fish, however, if it is of an appropriate size. You'll find it a real treat!

4–6 servings
450–600 g/1–1¼ lb whole whitemeat
  fish such as pomfret (*managatsuo*), sea bass
  (*suzuki*), red snapper (*tai*), or croaker
  (*ishimochi*)(1 fish per serving)
⅓ leek, cut into thin strips
2 slices fresh ginger root
Seasonings:
  ½ teaspoon sugar
  ½ teaspoon salt
  1 tablespoon saké
  1 teaspoon shoyu

Sauce:
  ½ cup broth from the steamed fish
  Pinch of sugar
  ½ teaspoon salt
  Dash of pepper
  2 teaspoons saké
  1 teaspoon shoyu
¼ leek, cut into fine strips
3 slices fresh ginger root, cut into thin strips
1 tablespoon salad oil
5 sprigs of *mitsuba* trefoil, cut into 5 cm/2 inch
  lengths

1 Scale and gut the fish. Score both sides of the fish crosswise at 2 cm/1 inch intervals.
2 Place leek strips and ginger strips in a dish which is large enough for the fish and add the fish.
3 Mix the seasonings and sprinkle them over the fish. Steam in a steamer over high heat for 15 minutes.
4 Pour the broth from the steamed fish into a small sauce pan and add the rest of the ingredients for the sauce. Bring to a boil and pour over the fish. Garnish with *mitsuba* trefoil before serving.

Chilled Seafood and Tofu in Plum Sauce

(Hiyashi bachi)

Chilled dishes like this one are especially appreciated during Japan's hot, humid summers.

The sauce, which is made from pickled plums (*ume-boshi*), is usually served with chilled sea-snake (*hamo*) dishes when summer festival season comes around in the Osaka-Kyoto area. The sour taste stimulates the appetite, and it feels refreshingly cool on the palate.

4 servings
Plum Sauce:
  3 large pickled Japanese plums (*ume-boshi*), cored and chopped
  10 green *shiso* leaves, chopped
  4 tablespoons *dashi* stock, see page 129
  1 teaspoon sugar
  2 tablespoons mirin
  2 teaspoons shoyu
1 fresh squid (*ika*)
8 shrimp
½ teaspoon salt
1 tablespoon saké
3 cups boiling water
Ice water to chill the seafood
Ice cubes for serving
1 cake soft tofu (*kinugoshi-dofu*), cut into 8 pieces
1 small Japanese cucumber, pulp removed and cut into 12 thin rings
8 fresh or 4 canned cherries

1 Place the ingredients for the Plum Sauce in a food processor, and blend until the sauce is smooth and creamy. Chill until serving.
2 Gut and skin the squid. Cut the squid lengthwise down the center and open it up. Carefully score the skin side in a checkered pattern with lines at 3 mm/⅛ inch intervals, holding the knife at a 30° angle above the squid.
3 Devein and cut off the tips of the shrimp tails.
4 Add the salt and mirin to 3 cups of boiling water in a pot, cook the squid and shrimp quickly, and dip them in ice water to chill. Drain well and shell the shrimp, leaving the tails on.
5 Cut an opening in 4 cucumber rings and link 2 other rings to each of them.
6 In a large glass bowl, arrange ice cubes, tofu, squid, shrimp, cucumber rings and cherries. Serve with the plum sauce.

Pan-Teriyaki for Yellowtail Fish

(Buri no Nabe-teriyaki)

This is my variation of teriyaki using a pan instead of skewers or a broiler. This is much easier than the traditional method of making teriyaki, in which a fish is marinated in a special teriyaki sauce for 30 minutes and broiled on skewers. The traditional broiling method requires a great deal of skill, as fish meat cooked this way will separate easily and can be seared from sauce and oil that drip from the fish onto the heat source.

4 servings
Teriyaki Sauce:
  1 tablespoon sugar
  2 tablespoons saké
  2 tablespoons mirin
  4 tablespoons shoyu
1½ tablespoons salad oil
12 Japanese green peppers (*shishito*)
Pinch of salt
4 fillets, 100 g/¼ lb each yellowtail (*buri*)

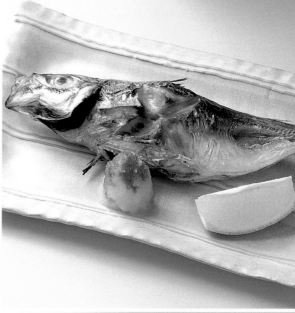

1 Place the sauce ingredients in a saucepan and bring to a boil.
2 Heat 1 tablespoon salad oil in a frying pan and sauté the green peppers. Sprinkle with salt.
3 Heat a frying pan until it starts to smoke. Grease the pan with the remaining salad oil. Place the fish in the pan, and sauté on both sides, skin side first, over medium heat until done. Shake the pan occasionally to prevent sticking.
4 Discard the oil from the pan. Raise the heat, pour in the sauce, and cook until the fish is evenly coated with sauce, shaking the pan gently but frequently. When the sauce thickens, remove from the heat and arrange the fish and green peppers on individual serving plates.

Salt-Broiled Fish

(Sakana no Shioyaki)

This is one of the simplest ways to cook fish but one of the best ways to appreciate its special flavor. The Japanese, like some Europeans, like to eat fish this way when the fish is really fresh. You'll find it well worth a try.

4 servings
4 fillets of any kind of fish, or 4 small fish per
  serving
2 teaspoons salt
10 cm/4 inch lengths of *daikon* radish,
  peeled and grated
Shoyu
4 lemon wedges

1 Sprinkle both sides of the fish with salt from about 30 cm/1 foot above so that the fish is evenly salted. Let stand for 30 minutes or until brine runs from the fish.
2 Skewer two fish fillets apiece with two or three metallic skewers. (When a whole fish is used, skewer from the mouth toward the tail.)
3 Place a fish broiler over high heat. Broil the fish on the skin side first until 60% done, keeping it 10 cm/4 inches from the broiler, then turn over and broil completely on the other side.
   Alternative: If a fish broiler is not available, heat and grease a frying pan and sauté the fish on both sides, with the skin side first.
4 Serve with grated *daikon* radish and shoyu. Lemon wedges are also a good accompaniment.

Salting: The amount of salt to use depends on whether the fish is white fish or a dark-skinned oily fish, and also on the thickness of the fillet. Oily fish or thicker fillets need more salt. Use salt equivalent to about 2% of the fish weight, or ½ teaspoon salt for a fillet of fish weighing 100 g/¼ lb.

Broiling utensils: There are several utensils that can be used to broil fish (see page 125). A set including a flame expander (*yakiami*), skewer holder (*tetsukyu*) and skewers (*kanagushi*) is best, though expensive. They last a lifetime, however, if you replace the flame expander every few years. The net for broiling fish shown in photo is handy, and it brings the fish close to the heat source. Before you broil, you should heat the broiling utensil until almost red to prevent sticking.

Fish Boiled in Sauce

(Ni-zakana)

For this recipe almost any kind of fish can be used, including white fish or dark-skinned oily types. Should you have a day-old fish which can no longer be eaten raw as *sashimi* or *sushi*, for instance, you should try boiling it as follows.

4 servings
Cooking Sauce:
  3 tablespoons sugar
  ½ cup saké
  ½ cup shoyu
  3 tablespoons mirin
  ¹/₂ cup water
4 fillets (100 g/¼ lb each) fish e.g. sea
  bream (*tai*), red snapper (*tai*), flounder
  (*hiramê*), turbot (*karei*), sea bass (*suzuki*),
  mackerel (*saba*), anglerfish (*anko*)
8 okra pods
  1 cup water to boil okra
  Pinch of salt

1 In a shallow pan, place the ingredients for the cooking sauce and bring them to a boil.
2 Place one layer of fish in the pan with the skin side up and set a drop lid (see page 41) or a piece of aluminum foil with a hole torn out of the center directly on top of the fish, so the cooking sauce covers the fish and seasons it evenly. Do not add all the fish fillets at the same time, but boil half of them separately. The boiling sauce will seal in the good taste of the fish.
3 Cook over medium high heat, reducing the heat as the cooking sauce decreases, until the sauce thickens and the fish is well-seasoned.
4 Boil the okra pods in water and salt just until they turn bright green, then plunge them into cold water to keep their color bright.
5 Arrange the fish and okra pods in individual serving plates. Serve warm.

CHICKEN & EGGS

Charcoal-Broiled Chicken on Skewers

(*Yakitori*)

The consistent heat generated by charcoal is ideal for this recipe. Most well-known *yakitori* restaurants in Japan use a special charcoal called *bincho*, made from the hard wood of an oak tree that grows in Wakayama prefecture.

Charcoal stoves are no longer commonly found in private kitchens, but a barbecue oven will suffice as an alternative. If you wish to make this recipe on your kitchen stove, you should use a pair of bricks or something similar in size that will not burn. Wrap each in aluminum foil and place on each side of the burner, keeping them far enough apart so that the skewers may be laid on them at either end. You may cover the tip of each skewer with aluminum foil to prevent them from burning.

4 servings
300 g/⅔ lb boneless chicken legs and thighs,
  cut into small bite-sized pieces
300 g/⅔ lb boneless chicken breast,
  cut into small bite-sized pieces
100 g/¼ lb chicken liver,
  cut into small bite-sized
  pieces
2 leeks, cut into 3 cm/1 inch
  lengths
12 Japanese green peppers,
  (*shishito*) seeded and cut
  into bite-sized pieces
Sauce Mixture:
  ½ cup mirin
  ½ cup shoyu
  ¼ cup saké
  1 tablespoon sugar
Bamboo skewers
Seven spices (*shichimi
  togarashi*), optional

1 Prepare the fire or other heat source for cooking the *yakitori*.
2 Put all the ingredients for the sauce into a small sauce-pan and boil for 1 minute. Pour into a large cup or other deep container.
3 Thread 2 or 3 chicken breast, leg and thigh pieces onto a skewer, alternating with the leek pieces. Repeat for the remaining pieces. Skewer the chicken liver pieces and the leeks separately. (Picture 1)
4 Broil the chicken and vegetables over direct heat, turning the skewers several times. Fan away the smoke with a hand-held fan, as the smoke from the burning fat can turn the chicken black and add a strong, smoky taste. When the chicken is cooked, dip it in the sauce to coat. Return it to the heat and broil for a while longer until it appears glazed. Dip the skewers in the sauce again and serve. Serve with seven spices, if desired. (Pictures 2–4)

Note:
Salt-broiled *yakitori*, seasoned by sprinkling only with salt just before broiling, is also quite tasty.

Store the leftover sauce in the refrigerator. The next time you make *yakitori*, add fresh sauce ingredients to the leftover sauce in the proportions listed in the recipe and boil. As the sauce ages, it mellows and becomes more flavorful.

Braised Chicken and Vegetables

(Iridori or Chikuzen-ni)

"Iridori" is literally translated as "sautéed chicken." The recipe originated in an area in western Japan called Chikuzen, as indicated by the other commonly used name for this recipe, "*Chikuzen-ni.*"

This is a traditional method of cooking chicken with a variety of fresh vegetables. All of the vegetables, except the green peas and *konnyaku*, are cut into portions of the same size, so that they can be cooked at the same time.

4 servings
1 block yam cake (*konnyaku*)
2 cups water for boiling *konnyaku*
2 tablespoons sesame oil
1 boneless chicken leg and thigh, cut into
  large bite-sized pieces
1 node lotus root (*renkon*), peeled and cut
  into bite-sized pieces
1 small burdock (*gobo*), with peel scraped off,
  cut into bite-sized pieces and dipped
  in cold water
1 small carrot, peeled and cut into bite-sized
  pieces
¾ cup *dashi* stock, see page 129
Seasonings:
  1 tablespoon sugar
  5 tablespoons light-colored shoyu
  ½ cup saké
  2 tablespoons mirin
¼ cup frozen green peas

1 Tear the *konnyaku* into bite-sized pieces with a spoon or by hand. Bring the water and *konnyaku* to a boil, then discard the water and continue cooking the *konnyaku*, while stirring, until its surface is dry.   (Picture 1)
2 Heat 1 tablespoon of sesame oil in a frying pan and sauté the chicken on both sides over high heat until nicely browned. The chicken need not be completely cooked at this point.

3 Add the *konnyaku*, lotus root, burdock and carrot and stir-fry until all of the ingredients in the frying pan are evenly coated with oil.
4 Add the stock and seasonings, cover with a drop lid and cook for 20 minutes. Shake the pan occasionally while you cook to turn over the ingredients.   (Picture 3)
5 When the cooking sauce has nearly all been absorbed, sprinkle in the green peas and cook for an additional 2–3 minutes.   (Picture 4)

Drop lid (*Otoshi-buta*): This recipe calls for a drop lid, a wooden lid whose diameter is smaller than that of the pan so that it can be placed directly upon the ingredients. This ensures that even a small amount of sauce will cover the ingredients and season them evenly and thoroughly.

If you do not have a suitable drop lid, you may substitute aluminum foil. Cut or fold the foil into a circular shape slightly smaller than the mouth of the pan. To keep the foil stable so that it is not pushed upwards by the boiling sauce, cut a small hole, about 1 cm/½ inch in diameter, in the center of the foil.

One-Pot Cooking with Chicken and Vegetables

(Tori no Mizutaki)

This is one of the most popular *nabemono* (tabletop dishes) among the Japanese, particularly during the cold season. Just like *shabu-shabu*, for *mizutaki* a weak, kelp-based stock is used to cook chicken and vegetables. Try to select high-quality chicken.

4–6 servings
8 large Chinese cabbage leaves
30 g/½ lb spinach
Water for cooking the cabbage and spinach
1 whole (approximately 1.1 kg/2½ lb)
    chicken, cut up into small pieces
4 leeks, cut into 5 cm/2 inch lengths
1 cake hard tofu (*momen-dofu*), cut into 8 pieces
8 fresh *shiitake* mushrooms, the stem tips
    trimmed off
300 g/¾ lb *shungiku* chrysanthemum leaves,
    cut into 5 cm/2 inch lengths
50 g/2 oz dried potato noodles (*kuzukiri*)
Water for soaking the noodles

Condiments:
  5 cm/2 inch-long *daikon* radish, peeled,
    grated and drained in a colander
  1 teaspoon Japanese chili pepper paste
    (*yuzukosho* or *kanzuri*)
  4 green onions, finely chopped
Dipping Sauce:
  Juice from 1 Japanese *daidai* citrus or 3 limes
  3 tablespoons rice vinegar
  ½ cup Japanese stock, see page 129
  ½ cup shoyu
  2 tablespoons mirin
Cold water for cooking in the pot
10-square-cm/4-square-inch piece dried kelp
  for preparing stock (*dashi-kombu*)

1 Cook the Chinese cabbage in boiling water until limp. Drain and cool. Boil spinach in the same water just until limp. Put in cold water and quickly squeeze out liquid.
2 Spread 4 cabbage leaves on a bamboo mat used for rolling *sushi*. Place half of the cooked spinach atop the cabbage at the near end and roll up tightly. Do the same to the remaining cabbage and spinach. Cut the rolls crosswise at 2.5 cm/1 inch intervals.
3 Soak the potato noodles in boiling water for 10 minutes or until soft. Drain in a colander and place in cold water. Drain again.
4 Mix the grated *daikon* and chili pepper paste for condiments. Place each condiment in a small separate dish.
5 Arrange all the ingredients for cooking attractively on a large serving platter.
6 Mix the ingredients for the dipping sauce and pour into a sauce pitcher.
7 Fill an earthen pot (*donabe*) ¾ full with cold water and add the dried kelp.
8 Prepare the tabletop cooker and cook the broth over medium heat until almost boiling. Remove the kelp.
9 Add the chicken and bring to a boil, skimming off the bubbles that form. Add the mushrooms, leeks, tofu, chrysanthemum leaves, cabbage rolls and the noodles.
10 While waiting for the ingredients to be done, pour the dipping sauce into small individual serving bowls and let each person add the condiments of his or her choice.
11 Have each person take what he or she wants from the pot as it is cooked and dip it in the sauce. Cook the noodles briefly, with each diner add the amount he or she wants to the broth and warming it before eating.

Stewed Chicken and Chestnuts

(Tori to Kuri no Ni-mono)

When the fall comes, I enjoy fresh chestnuts in this way at least once during the season.

4 servings
2 tablespoons salad oil
450 g/1 lb chicken meat, legs and thighs, breasts, or both, cut into large bite-sized pieces
1 carrot, peeled and cut into leaf-shaped pieces
6 dried *shiitake* mushrooms, soaked soft in water and cut into bite-sized pieces, with soaking water retained for later use
12 small Japanese taro potatoes (*sato-imo*), skinned and parboiled
20 chestnuts, shelled, skinned and parboiled
Cooking Liquid:
   1¹/₂ cups *dashi* stock, see page 129, including the mushroom water
   3 tablespoons sugar
   3 tablespoons shoyu
   2 tablespoons mirin

1 cup fresh soybeans in the pod
Water to boil the fresh soybeans
1 teaspoon salt

1 In a stew pot, heat the salad oil and sauté the chicken pieces until brown. Add the carrot and mushrooms and stir for 1 minute.
2 Add the potatoes, chestnuts, and stock, and cook covered with a drop lid (see page 41) for 5 minutes. Add the sugar, salt, shoyu, and mirin, and cook until most of the cooking liquid is absorbed, turning the ingredients now and then by shaking the pot. Reduce the heat as the cooking liquid reduces.
3 In a pan, bring to a boil the soybeans, water, and salt, and cook over low-medium heat for 15 minutes. Remove the soybeans from the pan and shell them.
4 Place the stewed chicken and vegetables in a serving bowl and sprinkle with the soybeans before serving.

Maple-Colored Fried Chicken

(*Tatsuta-age*)

Tatsuta-age, fried chicken *Tatsuta* style, is named after an area called Tatsuta which used to be well-known for its brilliant maple leaves in the fall. The colorful coating of the *tatsuta-age* is reminiscent of autumn maple leaves..

4 servings
600 g/1⅓ lb fryer chicken, cut into bite-sized
  pieces
1 tablespoon ginger juice, see page 69
3 tablespoons saké
4 tablespoons shoyu

Chrysanthemum Turnips:
  4 small white turnips, peeled
  ½ teaspoon salt
Chili Pickling Marinade:
  1 dried red chili pepper (*taka no tsumé*),
    seeded and chopped
  1½ tablespoons sugar
  ½ teaspoon salt
  3 tablespoons rice vinegar

Japanese potato starch (*katakuri-ko*) to coat
  the chicken
Vegetable oil for deep-frying
8 green *shiso* leaves, washed and dried

1 Marinate chicken in the ginger juice, saké and shoyu for 30 minutes, stirring occasionally.
2 Chrysanthemum turnips: Score crosswise the turnips, deeply cutting them in close rows, but do not cut right through to the base. Sprinkle with salt and leave until the brine runs. Mix the ingredients for the chili pickling marinade and marinate the turnips in it for at least 10 minutes.
3 Dredge the chicken in the potato starch and leave 2–3 minutes so that the starch sticks completely to the chicken.
4 Heat oil at a low temperature, 160°C/330°F. Deep-fry the green *shiso* leaves until crispy, turning them over a few times.
5 Raise the temperature of oil to 180°C/365°F and deep-fry the chicken thoroughly until crispy. Drain off the oil.
6 On a serving plate, arrange the fried chicken, green *shiso* leaves, and turnips.

44

Steamed Chicken with Mustard Sauce

(Mushi-dori no Karashi Fumi)

4 servings
2 half-breasts chicken
½ teaspoon salt
2 tablespoons saké
Juice from ½ lemon
3 cabbage leaves, finely shredded
1 Japanese cucumber, cut into fine strips
¹/₃ carrot, cut into fine strips
Mustard Sauce:
  2 teaspoons prepared hot mustard
  2 tablespoons white sesame seeds, toasted
  and ground, see page 23
  1 teaspoon sugar
  ½ cup mayonaise
  2 teaspoons shoyu
Japanese *daikon* sprouts (*kaiware-na*), with roots
  removed, or a sprig of parsley for garnish

1 Sprinkle chicken with salt and saké and place in a heat-proof shallow dish.
2 Steam the chicken for 15 minutes or until succulent.
3 Sprinkle the chicken with lemon juice and slice diagonally into 1 cm/¹/2 inch-thick pieces.
4 Mix the cabbage, cucumber and carrot.
5 Blend the ingredients for the mustard sauce until smooth.
6 Arrange the chicken and the vegetables in a serving dish. Pour the mustard sauce over the chicken and garnish with *daikon* sprouts or parsley.

Fried Chicken Slices with Lemon Sauce

(Tori no Koromo-age)

4 servings
2 half-breasts chicken, sliced into
  5 x 7 cm/2 x 3 inch pieces
½ teaspoon salt
½ tablespoon saké
½ tablespoon shoyu
1 egg yolk
1 tablespoon Japanese potato starch
  (*katakuri-ko*)
1 tablespoon cold water
Dash of pepper
Coating Mix:
  5 tablespoons flour
  2 tablespoons Japanese potato starch
  (*katakuri-ko*)
Vegetable oil for deep-frying
Lemon Sauce:
  3 tablespoons sugar
  Juice from 1 lemon
  3 tablespoons cold water
  1¹/4 teaspoons salt
  2 teaspoons Japanese potato starch
  (*katakuri-k*o)
4 spears green asparagus, cut into
  5 cm/2 inch lengths
Pinch of salt
2 cups boiling water

1 Mix the chicken, salt, saké, shoyu, egg yolk, potato starch, water and pepper, and let stand for 30 minutes.
2 Mix the flour and potato starch and dredge the chicken pieces thoroughly in this mixture.
3 In a deep fryer, heat the vegetable oil to 180°C/365°F and deep-fry the chicken pieces until golden brown. Drain off the oil and arrange the chicken in a serving dish.
4 In a small saucepan, place the ingredients for the lemon sauce and bring to a boil, stirring constantly. Cook for 10 more seconds and pour it over the chicken.
5 Boil the green asparagus in salted boiling water for 1 minute, and drain.
6 Arrange the chicken and asparagus in a serving dish. Pour the lemon sauce over the chicken.

Rolled Omelet

(Dashi-maki Tamago)

My mother used to prepare this satisfying dish for me. It may appear simple, but producing a firm, nicely rolled omelet takes some skill. The knack will come with time, however, so keep trying.

4 servings
4 eggs
5 tablespoons *dashi* stock, see page 129
Seasonings:
  1-1½ tablespoons sugar
  ½ teaspoon salt
  1 teaspoon shoyu
Salad oil for greasing the pan

1 Beat eggs lightly in a mixing bowl to mix whites and yolks; do not overmix. Add stock and seasonings, and mix well.
2 Heat a rectangular rolled omelet pan or a skillet and grease it with a cheesecloth dipped in salad oil. Pour in enough of the egg mixture to thinly cover the surface of the pan. Cook until the top of the egg is almost dry. Using a spatula or chopsticks, roll up the egg towards you from the far end of the pan.   (Pictures 1–3)
3 Push the rolled omelet back to the far end of the pan. Pour in more egg mixture and lift up the rolled section as you do so, to have the egg

mixture cover the entire surface of the pan. Cook until the top of the egg is almost dried and roll the rolled section up towards you with the newly cooked egg.
4 Repeat the same process until you have cooked all of the egg mixture.   (Pictures 4–5)
5 Cut the omelet into slices 2 cm/¾ inch thick before serving.

Note:
The key to a well-rolled omelet is the temperature of the pan: If it is too low, the egg will be too soft and will be difficult to roll, but if the pan is too hot, the omelet will become hard and dry. Try to maintain a consistent, medium heat by reducing the flame or removing the pan from the heat at times.
  A rectangular Japanese omelet pan will allow you to roll perfectly-shaped oblong rolled omelets, like the ones you may see at *sushi* bars.
  If you are dissatisfied with the shape of your omelet, you can correct it by using a bamboo mat, as is used for making Rolled Sushi. If that is not available, you may substitute a piece of waxed paper large enough to wrap the omelet. Roll the omelet up tightly in either the mat or waxed paper while still warm. Leave it in the mat or paper until cool to set.

Steamed Egg Custard

(*Chawan-mushi*)

4 servings
12 fresh or canned gingko nuts
4 bite-sized pieces chicken
4 small shrimp, shelled and deveined
4 bite-sized pieces fish cake (*kamaboko*)
4 fresh *shiitake* mushrooms, stems removed
4 sprigs of *mitsuba* trefoil, tied in a loose knot
Egg Custard:
  3 eggs, well beaten
  2½ cups *dashi* stock, see page 129
  1 tablespoon light-colored shoyu
  1 teaspoon salt

1 Crack the shells of fresh gingko nuts using a garlic crusher or a nutcracker and shell them. Place the gingko nuts and water just to cover in a shallow pan and bring to a boil, stirring with the back of a ladle to remove the skin. Drain well. If you are using canned gingko nuts, just drain off the juice.

2 Put all the prepared ingredients except for the *mitsuba* in *chawan-mushi* bowls or in deep, oven-proof bowls, such as custard cups.

3 Mix the egg custard ingredients in a mixing bowl with a wire whisk. Beat until ingredients are mixed but not yet foamy. Strain. Divide egg custard into the bowls.

4 Place the bowls in a steamer, cover it with a towel and set a loose cover on top of the pan. Steam for 15 to 20 minutes over medium low heat. Lay the tied *mitsuba* on top of each custard 1 minute before it is done.

Note: If you are using an oven instead of a steamer, pre-heat the oven to 200°C/400°F. Arrange the bowls in a baking pan, pour hot water into the pan to ½ the height of the bowls, and cover loosely with aluminum foil. Bake for 5 minutes, reduce the heat to 160°C/320°F, and bake for 20 minutes. Lay the tied *mitsuba* on top 2–3 minutes before you finish baking.

Scrambled Eggs with Shrimp and Vegetables

(Ebi to Yasai no Iri-tamago)

4 servings
12 small shrimp
Pinch of salt
1 tablespoon saké
4 dried *shiitake* mushrooms, soaked soft
  in cold water and diced
½ small precooked bamboo shoot, diced
Seasoning Mix A:
  ⅔ cup *dashi* stock, see page 129
  ½ teaspoon salt
  2 teaspoons light-colored shoyu
  1 tablespoon mirin
1 tablespoon salad oil
Seasoning Mix B:
  ¼ teaspoon salt
  2 tablespoons sugar
  1 tablespoon mirin

4 eggs
4 tablespoons frozen green peas

1 Sprinkle salt and saké over the shrimp, stir with your fingers and set aside for 10 minutes to improve its aroma.
2 In a shallow pan, place the mushrooms, bamboo shoots and seasoning mix A and cook for 5 minutes over medium low heat. Add the shrimp and cook together until done. Drain off the cooking sauce.
3 In a flat pan, place the salad oil and seasoning mix B and stir to dissolve sugar and salt. Add the eggs and beat until the yolks and egg whites are mixed. Add the cooked ingredients and green peas and cook over low heat, stirring constantly but not too quickly, until the eggs stick together but are still slightly soft. Remove from heat but continue to stir for a short while. Serve immediately.

BEEF AND PORK

Sukiyaki

This dish is a perennial favorite at Japanese restaurants around the world. "Sukiyaki" literally means "to grill on a flat spade." It is said to have originated with farmers who hunted game or wild fowl and grilled their quarry in the fields on a wide-handled digging tool. A heavy-walled but shallow skillet is most suitable for cooking sukiyaki. Guests sit around the pot at the table and retrieve the ingredients from the pot as they are cooked, so a portable table stove using propane gas in a cylinder is especially handy.

Marbled beef cooked with shoyu and sugar may seem to some of us to be too high in salt and sugar from a health standpoint, but even today most people seem to enjoy sukiyaki as a festive treat. We still cook sukiyaki at my home when we have guests, and everyone who has tried the recipe below has liked it very much.

There is another aspect of sukiyaki cuisine that makes it extra-special: although Japanese women usually prepare all of the meals at home, with a sukiyaki meal their job ends at preparing the ingredients and arranging them on a platter. It's usually considered the man's job to cook sukiyaki at home (and often other *nabemono*, or one-pot dishes, as well).

4–6 servings
450–900 g/1–2 lb thinly sliced beef for sukiyaki
6 leeks, cut into 5 cm/2 inch lengths
1–2 cakes of broiled tofu (*yaki-dofu*),
cut into 8 pieces
450–600 g (1–1½ lb) yam noodles
 (*shirataki*), well-rinsed and cut into
 7 cm/3-inch lengths
100 g/¼ lb *enoki* mushrooms, with
 root section removed
100 g/¼ lb fresh *shiitake* mushrooms,
 cut in half after stems removed
200 g/½ lb *shungiku* chrysanthemum leaves,
 hard stems removed and leaves separated
1 cup wheat gluten cake (*fu*), soaked soft in cold
 water, then squeezed gently
1 piece beef suet
Seasonings:
 ½ cup sugar
 1 cup saké
 ½–⅔ cup shoyu
4–6 fresh raw eggs (at least one egg per person)

1 Arrange beef, leeks, broiled tofu, *shirataki*-noodles, mushrooms, chrysanthemum leaves and *fu* attractively on a serving platter, and set the seasonings out separately.
2 At the table, heat a sukiyaki pot and melt the suet, rubbing it atop the surface of the pot.
(Picture 1)
3 Sauté a few slices of beef until brown, sprinkling with sugar to prevent the meat from sticking to the pan. Add onion, broiled tofu, *shirataki* noodles and mushrooms and season with sugar, saké and shoyu, according to taste. Add the chrysanthemum leaves and wheat gluten cake later on, when you have more liquid in the pot, because the *fu* absorbs the liquid quite well.
(Pictures 2–3)

Continued on page 124.

Shabu-shabu

(Table-top Beef and Vegetables)

The beef for this dish is cut paper-thin, even thinner than sliced beef for sukiyaki. Store-prepared shabu-shabu beef is usually prepared with slices separated with pieces of thin plastic wrap so they will not stick together.

The cooking stock is prepared in a pot on a burner at the table. Guests select what they wish to eat from the prepared ingredients and cook them in the boiling stock, then dip the cooked food in the sauce of their choice and eat it.

The vessel used for shabu-shabu is a unique round copper pot with a chimney-shaped hollow portion in the middle. However, an earthenware pot (*donabe*) is often used as a substitute. Shabu-shabu is popular for several reasons. For one thing, although sukiyaki requires expensive well-marbled beef and uses sugar in cooking, regular red meat can be used for shabu-shabu. Even if it is not tender beef, the meat will be sufficiently tender because it is so thinly sliced. If the beef is marbled with fat, the fat will disappear when you dip the beef in the boiling stock before you eat it. In addition, the beef and other ingredients are cooked in a flavored but not highly seasoned soup stock, so you can flavor your food by dipping it in the sauce that you prefer.

4–6 servings
450–600 g/1–1½ lb beef, sliced paper-thin
  for shabu-shabu
5 Chinese cabbage leaves, cut into
  bite-sized pieces
4 leeks, cut into 5 cm/ 2 inch lengths
8 fresh *shiitake* mushrooms, with only tips
  of stems trimmed off, cut in halves
200 g/8 oz *enoki* mushrooms,
  roots trimmed off
1 cake hard tofu (*momen-dofu*), cut into
  bite-sized pieces
200 g/8 oz *shungiku* chrysanthemum leaves,
  hard stems removed and leaves separated
50 g/2 oz Chinese bean threads (*harusame*),
  soaked in boiling water to soften,
  rinsed in cold water, drained and
  cut into 10 cm/4 inch lengths
Cold water to fill ¾ of shabu-shabu pot
1 (10-cm/4-inch-square) piece of
  dried kelp for stock

Shoyu and Vinegar Sauce:
  ¼ cup Japanese rice vinegar
  ¼ cup mirin
  ⅓ cup shoyu
  2 tablespoons stock from shabu-shabu pot

Condiments for Shoyu and Vinegar Sauce:
  3 green onions, finely chopped
  4 tablespoons *momiji-oroshi* (grated *daikon*
    radish with dried red chili pepper; see below)

Sesame Sauce:
  ⅔ cup white sesame seeds, toasted and
    ground until pasty (see page 23)
  1 tablespoon Kyoto-style sweet *miso* paste
  ⅓ cup mirin
  ⅓ cup Japanese rice vinegar
  ½ cup shoyu
  ¼ cup stock from shabu-shabu pot

Author's Shabu-Shabu Sauce:
  ⅔ cup grated *daikon* radish
  1 cooking apple (*kogyoku*), peeled and grated
  1 clove garlic, minced
  2 teaspoons minced fresh ginger root
  ½ leek, finely chopped
  1 tablespoon minced parsley
  1 teaspoon sugar
  ¼ cup saké
  ⅓ cup Japanese rice vinegar
  ½ cup shoyu

1 First prepare the sesame sauce and one of the other two sauces, according to your taste preferences, by mixing together the ingredients as listed. Ladle the sauces separately into serving bowls, two bowls for each guest.
2 Prepare the other ingredients according to the instructions and arrange them attractively on a platter. Set the burner and a shabu-shabu pot three-quarters full of water on the table. Add dried kelp, bring to a boil, and remove the kelp just the water begins to boil.
3 Have each diner drop a slice of beef into the boiling stock, pick it up with chopsticks when cooked, dip it in the preferred sauce and eat.
4 Cook the Chinese cabbage, green onions, mushrooms and tofu in the boiling stock, and, as with the beef, dip them in sauce before eating. When cooking the bean threads, dip them in the boiling stock with your chopsticks for a few seconds and remove immediately. If they are dropped in the stock they may become too soft to pick up. You must scoop out the residue

from time to time to keep the stock clear and tasty. Guests may alternate adding beef and vegetables to the stock, or you may do as many shabu-shabu restaurants do and serve the beef first, and then the vegetables, to make the dish look most appetizing. Add water to the stock occasionally, as needed.

To make *momiji-oroshi*:
  5 cm/2 inch length *daikon* radish
  4 dried red chili peppers (*taka no tsumé*),
    seeded

Peel the radish, make four deep holes in the *daikon* radish with chopsticks or a skewer and insert a chili pepper in each hole. Grate the *daikon* radish and drain in a colander.
  Serve the sauce and *momiji-oroshi* in separate bowls.

Substitutes and shopping hints:

•Beef may be replaced by sliced pork or chicken. The Mongolians, who originated this dish, use mutton.

•You may substitute scallions for long green onions, sliced fresh button mushrooms for fresh *shiitake* mushrooms, and watercress for *shungiku* chrysanthemum leaves.

•Instead of making *momiji-oroshi*, or grated *daikon* radish, from scratch, you can use *kanzuri*, Japanese chili paste in a small jar that is available at Oriental groceries or in supermarket spice sections. Mix ½ teaspoon of the chili paste with grated and drained *daikon* radish for simply prepared *momiji-oroshi* that tastes as good as relish using whole peppers.

•Sesame seeds can be purchased more cheaply at an Oriental grocery or health food store than at the spice section of a supermarket. You may find them already toasted or even ground.

•Sesame paste in a jar is very convenient to use. Simply dilute the paste by gradually stirring in the liquid seasonings.

Semi-broiled Beef

(*Gyu no Tataki*)

You could call this Japanese-style roast beef. Since "oven roasting" is not a traditional Japanese cooking method, many non-urban Japanese only began enjoying the flavor of lightly broiled beef a decade or so ago. But it has rapidly gained popularity, and today you can easily find the dish on the menu at any drinking establishment. This particular recipe, however, is derived from a dish of bonito, a traditionally popular fish, that is cooked rare (*Tataki*).

4 servings
450 g/1 lb beef rump
1 clove garlic, sliced
½ teaspoon salt
Ice water for chilling the beef
1 bunch *daikon* sprouts or watercress
1 leek, cut into threads
Sauce:
  3 slices fresh ginger root, finely chopped
  2 green onions, chopped
  Juice from 1 lemon
  l tablespoon rice vinegar

3 tablespoons shoyu
1 tablespoon mirin

1 Rub the beef all over with the garlic slices and sprinkle with salt.
2 Skewer the beef with 3–4 metallic skewers and hold them at the ends in one hand.
3 Broil the beef over high heat until lightly browned.   (Picture above)
4 Plunge the beef on the skewers into ice water to cool. Chill in a refrigerator.
5 Mix the ingredients for the sauce.
6 Slice the beef thinly, arrange on a serving plate, and garnish with *daikon* sprouts and leeks. Pour the dipping sauce over the beef before serving.

Beef with Eggs and Burdock

(Gyuniku no Yanagawa)

Yanagawa is a well-known summer dish that is a favorite among Japanese men. This dish features eggs and small fresh-water fish called *dojo* —loach or mudfish. To me, though, this fish is not for eating. When I was a child staying with my grandmother in the country, *dojo* were my favorite playmates in the stream nearby.

I prefer to use beef instead of loach in this recipe. My family also finds this dish to be tastier than the original *yanagawa*, and I'm sure you will like it too. Cook Beef *Yanagawa* in a shallow pan, like a frying pan without a handle, or in a small earthenware pot (*donabe*).

4 servings
½ burdock (*gobo*)
1½ cups *dashi* stock, see page 129
Seasonings:
  ½ teaspoon salt
  1 tablespoon shoyu
  2 tablespoons saké
300 g/10 oz thinly sliced beef sirloin,
  cut into bite-sized pieces
3 eggs, beaten
Dashes of Japanese pepper powder
  (*kona-zansho*)
10 sprigs *mitsuba* trefoil, cut into 3 cm/1 inch
  lengths

1 Peel the burdock, rubbing its surface gently with the back of a knife. Pare into small, thin pieces in the same way as you would sharpen a pencil with a knife. Place the slices in cold water as you pare. Let stand until the water turns dark brown, then drain in a colander. Rinse under running water, and drain again in a colander.
2 Boil the *dashi* stock and seasonings in a shallow pan, add beef and burdock and cook for 2–3 minutes, or until the burdock is tender.
3 Pour the eggs over the beef and burdock, top with trefoil, cover, and cook over low heat until the eggs are almost set. Sprinkle with Japanese pepper and serve immediately.

Breaded Pork with Homemade *Tonkatsu* Sauce

(*Tonkatsu no Tezukuri Sosu Zoe*)

Tonkatsu, which literally means "pork cutlet," is a Japanese version of Wiener Schnitzel. It is very popular among the foreign residents in Tokyo as well as among the Japanese. This dish is an outstanding Japanese pork specialty.

4 servings

Homemade *Tonkatsu* Sauce:
  2 tablespoons salad oil
  1 onion, finely chopped
  ½ carrot, finely chopped
  1 clove garlic, minced
  2 teaspoons minced fresh ginger root
  1 teaspoon curry powder
  2 tablespoons tomato paste
  1 tablespoon fruit chutney
  1 cube consomme beef bouillon
  1¼ cups water
  2 tablespoons Worcestershire sauce
  Dash of black pepper
4 fillets, each 1 cm/½ inch thick, pork loin

½ teaspoon salt and dash of pepper
Flour for dredging
1 egg, lightly beaten
Bread crumbs for coating
Vegetable oil for deep-frying
4 cabbage leaves, finely shredded
1 lemon, cut in half, then sliced

1 First make the *Tonkatsu* Sauce. Heat oil in a sauce pan and sauté all the chopped vegetables until tender, then add the remaining ingredients, stirring frequently. Simmer uncovered for about 30 minutes, stirring occasionally while it thickens. This sauce can be kept in a refrigerator if it is reboiled once a week, or it may be frozen.
2 Cut off the strings of the pork fillets along the edges between the fat and the flesh using the back of a knife, to prevent curling when cooked.
3 Pound the pork lightly with a meat mallet. Salt and pepper the cutlets, and dredge throughly in flour.
4 Dip in egg, and coat with bread crumbs.
5 Heat oil to 180°C/365°F in a frying pan or skillet and fry the pork until golden brown and crisp on the surface, turning over once.
6 Arrange the *tonkatsu*, shredded cabbage and lemon slices on plates, and serve with the sauce.

Ginger Pork

(Buta no Shoga-yaki)

These pork slices sautéed in a ginger-based sauce are a lunch-time favorite in Tokyo. Most restaurants cut slightly thicker slices because they look better. But I prefer somewhat thinner slices, since they absorb the ginger juice and sauce better.

4 servings
Seasonings:
  1½ tablespoons ginger juice, see page 69
  1½ tablespoons saké
  1½ tablespoons shoyu
450 g/1 lb thinly sliced pork loin
3 tablespoons salad oil
4 lettuce leaves, torn into bite-sized pieces
4 sprigs of parsley

1 Combine the ginger juice, saké and shoyu in a mixing bowl and rub this mixture onto the pork slices until all the liquid is completely absorbed.   (Picture above)
2 Heat 1 tablespoon of salad oil in a frying pan or a skillet, and add one layer of pork slices. Sauté both sides over high heat until brown. Remove from the pan and keep warm.
3 Cook the remaining pork in the same way. Arrange on serving plates lined with lettuce. Garnish with parsley sprigs and serve immediately.

Note: The pork should not be left uncooked after being marinated, because the meat will get tough. Instead, you should sauté quickly after rubbing the meat lightly with the ginger juice and seasonings. Beef cooked this way is also tasty.

Golden Pork Sauté

(Butaniku no Kogane-yaki)

The word, *kogane* (golden) is usually used for a dish that looks yellow because of a coating of egg. This is easy to prepare and delicious. My sister-in-law, who doesn't cook much, says that she makes it when she has to cook something but no dishes come readily to mind. Most people like its taste, as I can tell from my class experience.

4 servings
Salt and pepper to taste
450 g/1 lb thinly sliced pork loin
3 eggs, beaten
3–4 tablespoons salad oil
1 lemon, cut in half then sliced
4 sprigs of parsley
Shoyu

1 Salt and pepper the pork on both sides and place in a shallow bowl. Pour in the beaten eggs and coat both sides of the pork.
2 Heat 1 tablespoon of salad oil and sauté the pork slices on both sides until they are browned to a golden yellow. Repeat the process, adding oil 1 tablespoon at a time, until the last slice of pork is done.
3 Arrange the pork, lemon and parsley on serving dishes and pass around the shoyu. Squeeze lemon juice and sprinkle shoyu over the pork as you eat.

58

Stewed Beef and Potatoes

(Niku-jaga)

This hearty dish is often called "Mom's home cooking" (*ofukuro no aji*). Frankly, I have no idea how many young mothers today know how to make it. Yet it remains a favorite recipe among Japanese and one of the most popular dishes on the menu at casual eating and drinking places. I often introduce it as a basic recipe.

4 servings
1 piece (2 tablespoons) suet
450 g/1 lb thinly sliced beef, cut into
  7 cm/3 inch lengths
300 g/⅔ lb yam noodles (*shirataki*),
  rinsed and cut into 7 cm/3 inch lengths
2 onions, sliced
5 potatoes, peeled and cut into 4–6 pieces
Cooking Liquid:
  5 tablespoons sugar
  ½ cup saké
  ⅓ cup shoyu
12 snow peas, with strings removed,

1 Heat a stewing pan, melt the suet and rub it around the inside of the pan. Sauté the beef until brown. If the meat sticks to the pan, sprinkle in a little sugar.
2 Add *shirataki* noodles, onions and potatoes, stirring well after each addition. Cover the pan and cook over medium heat for 5 minutes or until the edges of the potatoes turn translucent, shaking the pan several times.
3 Add the cooking liquid and put the lid back on. Cook for 20 minutes until most of the liquid is absorbed. Add the snow peas. Shake the pan gently several times while cooking but do not stir with a spatula or other utensil to avoid crumbling the potatoes.
4 Serve while hot.

Glazed Pork

(Ni-Buta)

4 servings
450 g/1 lb pork rump or shoulder meat
Cooking twine for pork
1 clove garlic
Marinade:
  2 teaspoons sugar
  1 tablespoon honey
  6 tablespoons saké
  6 tablespoons shoyu
  3 tablespoons mirin
  ½ leek, sliced
  Fresh ginger root, cut into 5 slices
  1 teaspoon Japanese peppercorns (*mi-zansho*)
    or black peppercorns
2 tablespoons sesame oil
2 tomatoes, cut into bite-sized pieces
3–4 leaves of bib lettuce
Prepared hot mustard

1 Bind the pork with twine into a symmetrical, rounded shape.
2 Cut the garlic clove into 2–3 pieces and rub the entire pork loin with them. Reserve the garlic to add to the marinade if you would like a stronger flavor.
3 Mix the ingredients for the marinade and marinate the pork for 3–4 hours. Turn the pork occasionally while marinating.
4 Heat the sesame oil in a thick-bottomed pan and sauté the pork, turning it so it browns evenly.
5 Add the remaining marinade to the pan, cover tightly with a lid and cook over medium heat for 25 minutes or until all the liquid is absorbed, turning the pork occasionally. Insert a skewer to check whether the pork is cooked; if the juice runs clear, it is done. Slice the pork thinly.
6 Arrange the pork slices, lettuce and tomatoes on a serving plate. Serve hot or cold with mustard.

VEGETABLES AND TOFU

Eggplant Country Style

(Nasu no Inaka-ni)

This is a stewed eggplant dish, which is simple to prepare but is rich in flavor. This is good warm or cold.

4 servings
8 Japanese eggplants, halved lengthwise
3 tablespoons salad oil
1 dried red chili pepper (*taka no tsumé*), seeded
  and chopped
1 cup dried bonito flakes (*kezuri-bushi*),
  unpacked
Seasonings:
  4 tablespoons sugar
  3½ tablespoons shoyu
  2 tablespoons mirin
1 cup water

1 Score the eggplant skins diagonally.
(Picture 1)
2 Heat oil in a large pan and add the eggplants and red chili pepper. Cover quickly, and turn the eggplants by shaking the pan so they are even-ly coated with oil. Add bonito flakes, the sea-sonings and water. Cover with a drop lid (see page 41) or with a piece of aluminum foil, fold-ed to cover the ingredients with a small hole cut out of the center, and then the regular lid. Reduce the heat to medium low, and cook for 20 minutes, shaking the pan occasionally until most of the liquid is absorbed and the eggplants are well-seasoned. Serve hot or cold.

(Pictures 2–5)

Note: If the eggplants are small, use a few more and score lengthwise all around at 5 mm/⅕ inch intervals, instead of cutting in half.

Beef and Lotus Root

(Gyuniku to Renkon no Itame-ni)

1 medium length, about 200 g/½ lb
   lotus root
2 tablespoons salad oil
1 onion, sliced
200 g/½ lb ground beef
1 tablespoon shoyu
5 slices fresh ginger root
5 tablespoons frozen green peas
Seasonings:
   2 tablespoons sugar
   4 tablespoons water
   1½ tablespoons shoyu
   ½ teaspoon salt
   2 tablespoons mirin

1 Peel the skin off the lotus root thinly with a vegetable peeler. Cut in half lengthwise and slice into 8 mm/⅓ inch thick pieces. Dip in cold water as you slice, rinse under running water, and drain in a colander.

2 Heat salad oil in a pan, sauté the onion until soft, add the beef and ginger and stir-fry until the beef is brown. Add the lotus root and green peas and stir-fry for a while. Add the seasonings, cover the pan, and cook over medium heat until the liquid is absorbed, turning over the ingredients several times.

Tricolor Stir-Fried and Boiled Vegetables

(Sanshoku Kimpira)

To those who might think that "Stir-Fried Burdock" (*Kimpira gobo*) is an unexciting dish, I recommend that you try this recipe of my own creation, which combines a few other ingredients which go very well with burdock. I cook a large quantity of it and keep it in the refrigerator for several days so that I can serve it as a side dish for informal meals.

6–8 servings
1 burdock (*gobo*), washed
1 yam cake (*konnyaku*), cut into matchsticks
Water to boil yam cake (*konnyaku*)
2 tablespoons salad oil
1 or 2 dried red chili peppers (*taka no tsumé*) seeded and chopped
1 carrot, cut into matchsticks

Seasonings:
½ cup *dashi* stock, see page 129
1½ tablespoons sugar
4 tablespoons shoyu
3 tablespoons mirin
2 teaspoons sesame oil

1 Scrape the skin off the burdock with a wire brush or the back of a knife. Cut it into matchsticks and dip in cold water as you cut. Keep it in the water until the water turns dark. Rinse a few times and drain in a colander.
2 Place the yam cake and water to cover in a pot, bring to a boil, and drain. Put the yam cake back into the pot and cook, stirring occasionally, until it begins to crackle.
3 Add the salad oil, red chili peppers, burdock, and carrot and stir-fry. Add the seasonings. Cover the pot and cook over medium heat, stirring occasionally until most of the cooking sauce is absorbed. Sprinkle on sesame oil before turning off the heat.

Suprême Pumpkin

(Kabocha no Tsuya-ni)

This makes a tasty accompaniment to a meat dish as well as a vegetable side dish. This dish has always been very popular with my Western students.

4 servings
450 g/1 lb Japanese pumpkin, seeded
  and cut into about 3 cm/1 inch cubes
Water for cooking pumpkin
3 tablespoons butter
4 tablespoons sugar
1 teaspoon salt

1 Put the pumpkin, enough water just to cover, butter, sugar and salt in a pan, cover the pan and cook over a high heat until boiling. Lower the heat to medium, and then to low as the cooking liquid reduces. Cook until the liquid is absorb-ed.
2 Serve while hot.

Variation:
This dish combining pumpkin and adzuki beans is called *itoko-ni,* which means "boiled cousins." I don't know why it was thought that pumpkin and adzuki beans are that closely related. At any rate, they are indeed well matched in this dish.

Pumpkin and Adzuki Beans
(*Itoko-ni*)

4 servings
600 g/1½ lb Japanese pumpkin
2 cups *dashi* stock, see page 129
3 tablespoons sugar
¾ teaspoon salt
2 teaspoons shoyu
2 tablespoons mirin
1 can (300 g/⅔ lb) boiled adzuki beans

1 Seed the pumpkin and cut into chunks.
2 Put the pumpkin, stock, sugar, salt and shoyu in a pan and cook over medium heat for 15–20 minutes until the pumpkin is soft.
3 Add mirin and adzuki beans and cook for 15 minutes until the cooking sauce thickens. Reduce the heat gradually as the cooking sauce reduces and gets thicker.

Spring Onion and Fried Tofu Salad

(Wakegi to Aburage no Nuta)

4 servings
300 g/10 oz spring onions (*wakegi*), cut into
    5 cm/2 inch lengths
  Boiling water for cooking onions
1 teaspoon salt
2 sheets thin-fried tofu (*aburage*)
  Boiling water to pour over fried tofu
Miso Dressing:
  3 tablespoons white sesame seeds, toasted
    and ground to a powder, see page 23
  4 tablespoons Kyoto-style sweet *miso* paste
    (*saikyo-miso*)
  1 tablespoon sugar
  1 tablespoon mirin
  2 tablespoons rice vinegar
  1 tablespoon *dashi* stock, see page 129

1 Cook the spring onions in salted boiling water for a few minutes and drain in a colander until cooled.
2 Place the thin-fried tofu in a colander and pour boiling water over them, turning them over and repeating the process on the other side to remove excess oil. Squeeze out water by lightly pressing with a chopstick atop the fried tofu and rolling it across the surface. Cut the fried tofu into narrow strips.
3 Mix ingredients for the *miso* dressing. Add onions and thin-fried tofu and mix thoroughly before serving.

Snow Peas Mimosa-Style

(Saya-endo no Tamago-toji)

The combination of green (snow peas) and yellow (eggs) reminds us of the clustered yellow flowers and green leaves of the mimosa tree.

4 servings
300 g/⅔ lb snow peas
2 sheets thin-fried tofu (*aburage*), shredded
1 cup *dashi* stock, see page 129
2 tablespoons sugar
2½ tablespoons light-colored shoyu
2 tablespoons mirin
2 eggs, beaten

1 Remove the strings from both sides of the snow pea pods. Heat the stock in a pan.
2 Cook the snow peas and fried tofu in the stock until the pea pods turn bright green. Add seasonings and cook for 5 minutes, uncovered.
3 Stir in the eggs, cover the pan and simmer until the eggs are almost set.

Variation:
Green Peas and Snow Peas with Eggs
(*Grinpisu to Saya-endo no Tamago-toji*)

4 servings
1¼ cups *dashi* stock, see page 129
1 cup fresh green peas (300 g/⅔ lb when in the pod)
2 cups snow pea pods (200 g/8 oz)
1 tablespoon mirin
½ teaspoon salt
1 tablespoon shoyu
2 eggs, beaten

1 In a shallow pan, place the stock and green peas, and cook covered for 5–7 minutes over medium-low heat, until the peas are soft.
2 Add the snow peas and cook until the pods turn bright green in color.
3 Add sugar, salt, mirin and shoyu and raise the heat to medium-high. Cook 2 more minutes.
4 Pour eggs over the peas and pods, and reduce the heat to low. Cover the pan and simmer until the eggs set.
5 Divide into 4 serving bowls and serve right away.

Note: This dish is good both warm and cold.

Sesame Green Bean Salad

(Ingen no Goma-ae)

4 servings
300 g/⅔ lb fresh green beans
4 cups water to boil beans
Pinch of salt
Sesame Dressing:
   3 tablespoons white sesame seeds, toasted
      and ground, see page 23
   2 tablespoons *dashi* stock, see page 129
   1½ tablespoons shoyu
   2 tablespoons mirin

1 Remove the strings from both sides of the green beans, snapping off both ends. Cut into 5 cm/2 inch lengths.
2 Boil water in a pot with a pinch of salt, add string beans, and boil for 3–5 minutes or until soft. Do not overcook. Drain in a colander.
3 Mix the ingredients for the sesame dressing in a mixing bowl. Add the beans and toss thoroughly until well-coated. Serve while still warm.

Variation:
Sesame Spinach Salad
(*Horenso no Goma-ae***)**

This is another popular Japanese salad. You can cook many other green leafy vegetables besides spinach in the same way with the sesame dressing.

4 servings
5 cups water to boil spinach
350 g /12 oz fresh spinach, washed and cleaned
Sesame Dressing:
   3 tablespoons white sesame seeds, toasted
      and ground, see page 23
   2 tablespoons *dashi* stock, see page 129
   2 tablespoons shoyu
   1 tablespoon mirin

1 Boil water in a pan, add spinach and again bring to a boil. Remove the spinach and dip in cold water to cool, then squeeze out water. This procedure must be done quickly, or the spinach will lose flavor and nutrients. Cut the spinach into 4 cm/1½ inch lengths.
2 In a mixing bowl, mix the sesame seeds and the seasonings. Add the spinach and mix well just before serving.

66

Sesame Salad with Cucumbers and Mushrooms

(Kyuri to Shiitake no Goma-zu-ae)

4 servings
2 Japanese cucumbers, thinly sliced
1 teaspoon salt
8 fresh *shiitake* mushrooms
10 green *shiso* leaves, shredded
Sesame Dressing:
  3 tablespoons white sesame seeds, toasted
    and ground, see page 23
  1 tablespoon sugar
  2 tablespoons mirin
  1 tablespoon shoyu
  1 tablespoon rice vinegar

1 Sprinkle cucumber slices with salt and mix well. Let stand for 10 minutes, then squeeze out the brine.
2 Trim off the ends of the mushroom but leave the stems on. Broil on both sides over low, direct heat until done, using a small, square grill. The mushrooms should be reduced in size, soft and succulent. Cut them into narrow strips, and cool.
3 Mix all the ingredients for the sesame dressing thoroughly and toss with the vegetables right before serving.

Variation:
Salad with Cucumbers and Japanese Pears
(Kyuri to Nashi no Sarada)

4 servings
2 Japanese cucumbers, cut into fine strips
  ½ teaspoon salt
1 Japanese pear (*nashi*), pared, quartered,
  cored and cut into fine strips
Dressing:
  4 slices fresh ginger root, finely chopped
  2 round tablespoons chopped leek
  2 teaspoons sugar
  Pinch of salt
  3 tablespoons rice vinegar
1 teaspoon white sesame seeds, toasted

1 Sprinkle cucumbers with salt and mix well. Let stand for 5 minutes and squeeze out lightly. Mix cucumbers and pears in a salad bowl.
2 Mix the ingredients for the dressing and pour over the salad. Toss lightly and chill until serving.
3 Serve the salad topped with the sesame seeds.

Sesame Burdock Salad

(Tataki Gobo)

This dish is traditionally prepared for New Year's Day. Its name, *tataki gobo* (pounded burdock), refers to the process of pounding the burdock sticks to soften them.

8–10 servings
2 sticks burdock
6 cups water to boil burdock
2 tablespoons rice vinegar
Sesame Dressing:
  4 tablespoons white sesame seeds, toasted
    and ground, see page 23
  ½ cup *dashi* stock, see page 129
  1 tablespoon light-colored shoyu
  2 tablespoons mirin
  2 tablespoons rice vinegar

1 Wash the dirt from the burdock sticks, scrape the skin with the back of a knife, and cut into 25 cm/10 inch long pieces. Quarter thick sticks lengthwise and halve sticks of medium width; sticks of equal width will take the same amount of time to cook. While you cut them, dip the ends in cold water and let them soak until the water turns brown. Wash the burdock under running water.
2 Boil water and the vinegar in a big pan, add the burdock, and boil for 10 minutes, until soft but still crunchy.
3 Drain the burdock and spread the sticks out on a cutting board. Sprinkle with salt and tap with a Japanese grinding stick, a rolling pin or the side of a cooking knife. This loosens the burdock fibers and enables them to easily absorb flavor. Cut them into 5 cm/2 inch long pieces.
4 Mix the ingredients for the sesame dressing in a mixing bowl, add the burdock and toss thoroughly until well-coated. This salad will keep for several days if refrigerated.

Note: If you use a Japanese mortar and pestle to grind the sesame seeds, add the other ingredients to the mortar and dress the beans in this mixture. Frozen or canned string beans are not suitable for this recipe as they lack firmness and flavor.

Tofu Steak with Mushroom Sauce

(Tofu no Suteki Kinoko Sosu)

2 cakes of hard tofu (*momen-dofu*), wrapped
in paper towels to drain for 30 minutes
(Picture 1)

Seasoning Mixture:
  1 tablespoon shoyu
  1 tablespoon Japanese potato starch
    (*katakuri-ko*)
  1 tablespoon water
2 tablespoons salad oil
4 tablespoons butter
200 g/½ lb *shimeji* mushrooms, stems
  removed and separated into bunches of
  2 to 3 stems each
Mushroom Sauce:
  1 tablespoon shoyu
  3 tablespoons white wine
  Salt and pepper to taste
  3 tablespoons fresh cream

1 Cut the tofu in half.
2 Mix the ingredients for the seasoning mixture.
3 Dip both sides of the tofu in the seasoning
sauce.   (Picture 2)
4 In a frying pan or skillet, heat 1 tablespoon
salad oil and 2 tablespoons butter and sauté the
tofu slowly on both sides until nicely browned.
Place the tofu in individual serving plates.
(Picture 3)
5 Empty the pan, heat the
remaining oil and butter and
sauté the mushrooms. Add
shoyu, salt, pepper and wine,
and cook for 1 minute. Stir in
cream and spoon the sauce
with the mushrooms over the
tofu.   (Picture 4)

Preparing Ginger Juice

1 Pare the skin off a piece of ginger root
with a knife.   (Picture 1)
2 Grate the skinned ginger into a small
cooking bowl lined with a cheesecloth.
(Picture 2)
3 Gather the corners of the cheesecloth
together and squeeze the juice into a bowl.
(Picture 3)

Chilled Tofu

(Hiya-yakko)

4 servings
2 cakes of soft tofu (*kinugoshi-dofu*), chilled
2 teaspoons grated fresh ginger root
1 sheet, about 20 x 20 cm/8 x 8 inch toasted
   nori laver, cut into fine strips
1 tablespoon shoyu

This is the easiest and simplest way of serving tofu, but most Japanese just love it. They like their tofu chilled, especially in the heat of summer. The *hiya* in *hiya-yakko* actually means "chilled."

When you eat uncooked tofu which you buy at a tofu shop or from a street vendor who sells tofu door-to-door, I recommend that you first boil it to sterilize the tofu. This is because vendors keep tofu in water, and they scoop it up with hands that may have touched other things.

To boil tofu: Place the tofu, cold water to cover, and a pinch of salt in a pot and bring to a boil. Turn off the heat and let it stand until cool, then refrigerate. Never overcook or tofu will become spongy and too firm.

1 Place one cake of soft tofu on your palm and cut it into 8 pieces. Divide them into two individual serving bowls. Do the same with the other cake of tofu to prepare four bowls of tofu.
2 Set an equal amount of grated ginger atop each serving of tofu. Crumble the toasted *nori* laver and sprinkle it over the tofu. Add a dash of shoyu and serve immediately.

Alternative toppings: Dried bonito flakes (*kezuri-gatsuo*) or chopped chives or green onions may be good replacements or added toppings. When in season, fresh *yuzu* citrus rind or *sudachi* lime juice are also good accompaniments to fresh tofu.

Tofu and Mushroom Soup in a Pot

(Ni-yakko Dofu)

Japanese earthenware pots, or *donabe*, keep the foods which are cooked in them warm for a long time. A *donabe* is an essential utensil for one-pot cooking, or *nabemono*. If you prepare this dish in a *donabe* and serve it as is at the table, it will usually keep the food warm until you're finished eating.

4 servings
3 cups *dashi* stock, see page 129
1 teaspoon salt
2 tablespoons shoyu
100 g/4 oz *shimeiji* mushrooms with roots removed, separated into bunches of 2 or 3 stems
150 g/6 oz *enoki* mushrooms, ends cut off and stems cut in halves
2 cakes of hard tofu (*momen-dofu*), drained and diced
50 g/2 oz *shungiku* chrysanthemum leaves, leaves separated from the stalks
2 eggs, beaten
1 green onion, chopped
2 large pieces toasted *nori* laver, crumbled

1 In an earthenware pot (*donabe*), bring the *dashi* stock, salt and shoyu to a boil.
2 Add the mushrooms and tofu and cook until boiling again.
3 Add the chrysanthemum leaves and pour in the eggs in thin streams atop the other ingredients.
4 Sprinkle the green onion on top, cover the pot and turn off the heat. Let stand a few minutes before serving and serve with the *nori* laver.

Apple and Persimmon Salad with Tofu Dressing

(Ringo to Kaki no Shira-ae)

This Japanese-style salad includes a traditional tofu dressing. With its two seasonal fruits, apples and persimmons, this particular salad tastes almost like a dessert, so it has always been very popular among my students. This dressing may also be used with many other vegetables.

4 servings
1 small cooking apple (*kogyoku*)
1 cup cold water to soak apple
Pinch of salt
1 large persimmon
Sesame-Tofu Dressing:
  2 tablespoons white sesame seeds, toasted, see page 23
  ½ cake of hard tofu (*momen-dofu*), drained by placing between 2 flat dishes for 20 minutes
  ¼ teaspoon salt
  2 teaspoons sugar
  1 tablespoon mirin
  1 teaspoon light-colored shoyu
1 teaspoon minced *yuzu* citrus rind
Hama-bofu leaves for garnish

1 Quarter, core and dice the apple. Dip in salted water as you dice to prevent discoloration. Drain immediately in a colander.
2 Pare and dice the persimmon, removing any seeds.
3 For the dressing, grind the toasted sesame seeds in a Japanese mortar and pestle until pasty. (See note below). Add tofu and mix well. Add the salt, sugar, mirin and shoyu and mix to a smooth consistency.
4 Add the apple and persimmon and toss. Garnish with *hama-bofu* leaves and citrus rind.

Note: You can use an electric blender or a food processor instead of a mortar and pestle to grind the toasted sesame seeds and blend them with tofu and seasonings. Mix with the fruit in a mixing bowl.

Stir-Fried Tofu with Vegetables

(Iri-dofu)

4 servings
2 tablespoons salad oil
4 dried *shiitake* mushrooms, soaked soft
  in cold water, then shredded
½ carrot, cut into small matchstick-sized
  pieces
⅓ cup frozen green peas
3 tablespoons sugar
2 tablespoons shoyu
1 tablespoon mirin
2 cakes of hard tofu (*momen-dofu*)
2 eggs, beaten

1 Wrap the tofu in two layers of paper towel and let it stand for 5 minutes to drain.
2 Heat the salad oil in a frying pan, add the vegetables and stir-fry thoroughly over medium heat until the vegetables are wilted.
3 Add the seasonings and cook for 2 minutes. Add the tofu, and stir with a spatula, breaking the tofu into bite-sized pieces.
4 Raise the heat to high when the tofu and vegetables come to a boil, and stir in the eggs. Turn off the heat when the eggs are almost set.

Greens and Fried Tofu in Fish Stock

(Ao-na to Aburage no Nibitashi)

This recipe is usually cooked with stock from boiled and dried sardines (*niboshi*) rather than the more common Japanese stock made with kelp and bonito flakes. Should you find the taste to be a bit fishy, simply add a tablespoon of saké for a milder flavor.

4 servings
600 g/1½ lb *komatsu-na* or *kyo-na*, cut into
  5 cm/2 inch lengths
2 sheets thin-fried tofu (*aburage*), cut
  into 8 pieces
⅔ cup Japanese stock from boiled and
  dried sardines (*niboshi no dashi*; see page 131)
3 tablespoons shoyu

1 Boil the stock and fried tofu in a pot for 1 minute to extract the oil from the fried tofu. This will add flavor and counteract the bitter taste of the greens.
2 Add the white stems of the greens first, as they take longer to cook. When the stock is boiling again, add the green leaves, sprinkle with shoyu and cook, turning over several times until the leaves are soft but retain their bright green color.

Alternative: *Komatsu-na* is rich in vitamins A and C, minerals and calcium. Spinach, with its harsher flavor, is a poor substitute for *komatsu-na* in this recipe; Chinese cabbage would be a better alternative.

Rice & Noodles

Rice with Green Peas

(Ao-mame Gohan)

This rice is often cooked to celebrate the May 5th holiday of Children's Day, which was formerly called Boys' Day. The combination of green and white is thought to be appropriate for boys. My mother also cooked this rice for my brother's birthday on June 6th. It's a nice dish to try in May and June, when green peas are in season.

4–6 servings
3 cups rice, rinsed and drained, see page 128
3 cups plus 2 tablespoons cold water
3 cm/3-inch-square piece dried
  kelp *(dashi-kombu)*
⅔ cup fresh green peas
⅔ teaspoon salt
1 tablespoon mirin

1 Place the rice, water, dried kelp, green peas, salt and mirin in a heavy pot, and stir well. Let them stand at least 30 minutes.
2 Cover the pot and cook over medium heat until the liquid starts to boil. Raise the heat and cook for 2–3 minutes. Reduce the heat to low and simmer for 20 minutes. Raise the heat again to very high for 10 seconds, then turn off the heat.
3 Remove the kelp and quickly place a cooking towel or paper towels between the pot and the lid. Let stand it for 20 minutes.

Note: If you use an electric rice cooker, place all the ingredients in the cooker and let it sit for 30 minutes before turning it on. Stir it up gently when done.

Plain Rice *(Gohan)*

Rice has different names in Japanese depending on whether it is cooked or not. When it is not cooked, the grain is called *komé*. Once it is cooked, it is called *gohan*. *Gohan* also means a meal, indicating how important rice is to the Japanese as a staple food.

4 servings
2½ cups Japanese uncooked rice *(komé)*
2½ cups cold water

The following is the way we cook Japanese rice when an electric rice cooker is not available.

1 Wash rice in cold water, brisky rubbing it several times. Discard the milky water. Rubbing the grains together with your hands, repeat the washing process until the water runs clear. Drain the rice in a colander.
2 Put the rice into a thick, heavy pan, measure in an amount of cold water equal to that of the rice and let stand for at least 30 minutes. Cover and cook over medium low heat. Just before boiling, raise the heat. When boiling, reduce the heat to very low. Simmer for 20 minutes until all the liquid is absorbed. Raise the heat again, and cook for 10 seconds. Turn off the heat. Insert a paper towel between the pan and the lid. Let stand for 20 minutes before serving.

To cook rice in an electric rice cooker, measure the rice with the cup that came with the cooker. Wash and drain the rice and place the rice in the rice cooker. Add cold water according to the number of cups written on the side of the pan; if you are cooking 3 cups of rice, for example, add water until it reaches the line labeled 3 in the pan. Let stand for at least 30 minutes before you press the switch. When the rice cooker turns off automatically, the rice has been cooked and is ready to eat.

Chicken and Mushroom Rice

(Tori to Shiitake no Takikomi-gohan)

4 servings
2½ cups Japanese rice, rinsed and drained,
  see page 128
2½ cups *dashi* stock, see page 129
300 g/⅔ lb boneless chicken legs and
  thighs, diced
Seasoning Mix A:
  2 teaspoons shoyu
  2 teaspoons saké
2 thin-fried tofu (*aburage*), finely sliced
8 chestnuts, shelled, skinned and
  halved
8 fresh *shiitake* mushrooms with stem ends
  trimmed, sliced thinly

Seasoning Mix B:
  2 tablespoons saké
  5 tablespoons shoyu

1 Place the rice and stock in a heavy pot and let
stand for 30 minutes.
2 Sprinkle the chicken with seasoning mix A,
mix, and let stand for 10 minutes.
3 Add the chicken, fried tofu, chestnuts, mushrooms and seasoning mix B to the rice and mix
well.
4 Cover the pot and cook over medium heat
until boiling. Raise the heat to very high for half
a minute, reduce the heat to low and cook for 10
minutes. Reduce the heat to very low and simmer for 20 minutes, then raise the heat to very
high for 10 seconds. Turn off the heat and quickly insert a cooking towel between the pan and
the lid, so that the water sticking to the lid does
not drop on the rice. Let stand for 20 minutes
before serving.

Note: This dish is best cooked in a heavy pot atop
the stove. However, if you are using an electric rice
cooker, mix all the ingredients in the cooker after
Step 1. Turn on the switch. When the rice is done,
stir it gently. Let stand for 20 minutes.

Wooden rice container (*Ohitsu*)

Parent and Child *Domburi*

(*Oyako domburi*)

Oyako means "parent and child,"referring to this recipe's main ingredients of chicken and eggs. This is a very traditional *domburi* or dish of rice and toppings, and you can find it at almost any noodle restaurant.

4 servings
6 cups freshly boiled Japanese rice, see page 75
2 cups *dashi* stock, see page 129
Seasonings:
  1 teaspoon salt
  2 teaspoons shoyu
  1½ tablespoons mirin
1 boneless chicken leg and thigh, cut into
  bite-sized pieces
1 onion, thinly sliced
4 eggs, lightly beaten
10 sprigs of *mitsuba* trefoil, cut into
  3 cm/1 inch lengths

1 Divide rice evenly into 4 *domburi* bowls or soup bowls.
2 Mix the *dashi* stock, salt, shoyu and mirin, and pour ¼ of them into a small shallow pan.
3 Cook a quarter of the chicken and onion in a quarter of the stock until done. Pour a quarter of the beaten eggs in a thin stream atop the chicken. Add trefoil, cover the pan, and simmer until the egg is almost set.
4 Place the chicken and egg atop the rice in the bowl (see picture above). Repeat the same process for the other three servings.

Variations: If chicken is eliminated from this recipe, it becomes "egg *domburi*" (*tamago domburi*). Slices of laver are usually set on top of the egg. If chicken is replaced by beef, it is called *tanin domburi*. "*Tanin*" means persons unrelated to each other. Beef and egg are not relatives, much less parent and child.

Flower Garden *Sushi*

4–6 servings
Sushi rice:
  2 tablespoons sugar
  1 teaspoon salt
  5 tablespoons rice vinegar
  5 cups freshly boiled Japanese rice

8 shrimp, deveined
  Pinch of salt
  Seasoning:
    1 teaspoon sugar
    ¼ teaspoon salt
    2 tablespoons rice vinegar
5 slices boneless ham, finely chopped
5 green *shiso* leaves
2 tablespoons mayonnaise

4–5 dried *shiitake* mushrooms, soaked in
    water until soft and finely chopped, soaking
    water reserved.
⅔ cup *dashi* stock, see page 129
2 tablespoons sugar
1 tablespoon shoyu
1 tablespoon mirin

2 eggs
  Pinch of salt
  1 tablespoon mirin
  2 teaspoons salad oil

2 Japanese cucumbers, peeled
    and thinly sliced
  ½ teaspoon salt
  2 teaspoon sugar
  1 tablespoon saké

⅓ bunch *daikon* sprouts
  (*kaiware-na*), roots cut off
4 miniature tomatoes,
  cut in half

1 Mix well sugar, salt and vinegar until the sugar and salt are dissolved.
2 Place rice in a mixing bowl (flat wooden bowl if available) and sprinkle with the vinegar mixture. Mix quickly to season the rice evenly, fanning it to cool as quickly as possible.   (Picture 1)
3 Place the mushrooms in a pan with the soaking water. Bring to a boil and add sugar, shoyu and mirin. Cook over low heat until cooking liquid is absorbed, then cool to room temperature.
4 Fill a 21 cm/9 inch cake mold with a detachable base with half of the rice and flatten it gently at the top. (Picture 2) Cover the rice evenly with the mushrooms, then spread the remaining rice on top, flattening gently. Turn over onto a serving plate and remove the bottom, leaving the mold around the sides. Cover with a wet towel to prevent drying.
5 Cook the shrimp in boiling water with salt just until done and cool. Shell the shrimp, leaving the tails on. Mix the ingredients for the seasoning and sprinkle over the shrimp. Set it aside for 5 minutes.
6 Mix the ham, *shiso* leaves and mayonnaise.
7 In a small shallow pan, combine eggs, salt, mirin and salad oil and beat together. Cook slowly over low heat, stirring constantly to make soft scrambled eggs.
8 Rub cucumbers with salt in a colander and let them stand for 5 minutes. Squeeze out the brine of the cucumbers. Mix the sugar and saké and add to the cucumbers.
9 Unmold and uncover the rice and arrange the shrimp atop in the center. Place the eggs evenly around the shrimp and the ham mixture around it. Finish up with an outside ring of cucumber slices. Arrange *daikon* sprouts and tomato halves all around the *sushi* to garnish.
                    (Pictures 3–4)

Rolled *Sushi*

(*Norimaki*)

6 rolls:
4 cups Japanese uncooked rice
4 cups cold water
1 piece 10 x 10 cm/4 x 4 inches dried kelp
2 tablespoons saké

Vinegar Mixture:
  7 tablespoons Japanese rice vinegar
  6 tablespoons sugar
  1 tablespoon salt

Stuffing Ingredients:
50 g/2 oz dried gourd strips (*kampyo*),
  softened in cold water
  1 tablespoon salt
  2 cups *dashi* stock, see page 129
6 large dried *shiitake* mushrooms,
  soaked in water until soft
  5 tablespoons sugar
  1 teaspoon salt
  2 tablespoons shoyu
  2 tablespoons mirin
3 cakes freeze-dried tofu (*Koya-dofu*),
  softened in 60°C/140°F water
100 g/4 oz *mitsuba* trefoil, parboiled in salt water
3 eggs
  2 tablespoons sugar
  ¼ teaspoon salt

Vegetable oil to grease frying pan
6 sheets 20 x 20 cm/8 x 8 inches dried *nori* laver
50 g/2 oz pink sweet pickled ginger slices

1 Rinse the rice thoroughly and place it in a thick-walled, heavy pot, along with the water, kelp and saké. Let sit for at least 30 minutes before cooking.
2 Set the lid atop the pot. Cook the rice over medium-low heat until steam begins to rise from the pot, then raise the heat to high and cook until the liquid nearly boils over. Turn the heat down to very low and simmer for 20 minutes or until all the water is absorbed. Raise the heat again to very high for only 10 seconds. Remove the kelp and insert a thin towel between the pot and the lid. Remove from the heat and let sit for 5 minutes more.
3 Mix the ingredients for the vinegar mixture. Place the rice in a large wooden mixing bowl, if available, and quickly mix in the vinegar mixture to make *sushi* rice. Cover the bowl with a towel and cool to room temperature.
4 While the rice is cooking, rub the gourd strips with salt to partially soften them, then rinse off the salt. Cook the gourd in the stock for 20 minutes.
5 Remove the mushroom stems and place the mushrooms in the pan with the gourd strips. The stock should barely cover the ingredients; if the liquid is insufficient, supplement with the water used in soaking the mushrooms. Then add the sugar, salt, shoyu and mirin.
6 Rinse the freeze-dried tofu in running cold water, squeezing frequently between the palms. Then completely squeeze out the water. Add to the pan and cook together for 5 minutes. Cool to room temperature.
7 Beat the eggs gently to mix and season with sugar and salt. Lightly grease a frying pan with vegetable oil, then heat. Pour in the egg mixture, cover the pan and cook over low heat until the top of the egg is almost firm. Turn over with a spatula and cook the other side. Remove from the pan and cool to room temperature.
8 Cut all the cooked ingredients, except the *mitsuba* trefoil, into strips of the same width as the gourd strips
9 Place 1 sheet of *nori* laver on a bamboo rolling mat, with the glossy side down. Spread 1 cup of *sushi* rice evenly over the *nori* laver, leaving a 2.5 cm/1 inch border uncovered at the far edge of the *nori* laver. Arrange the cooked ingredients aligned crosswise in the middle of the *nori* laver, spanning from the right to the left side of the *nori*. (Pictures 1–2)

Continued on page 124.

Cold Buckwheat Noodles and Tempura

(Ten-zaru)

This recipe requires a degree of patience if you want to try it at home. Why? Because, ideally, both the tempura and the buckwheat noodles should be ready at the same time to enjoy the crispness of the tempura and the firm, smooth texture of the noodles. It may sound difficult, but I know from my classes that tempura soba is among the most popular Japanese noodle dishes among Westerners, so I decided to include this recipe here. I would recommend that you prepare this dish when you have a few extra hands to help out in your kitchen. Good luck!

4 servings
Dipping Sauce:
　2 cups cold water
　10 cm/4 inch length dried kelp
　1 cup thick bonito flakes
Seasonings:
　2 tablespoons sugar

1 tablespoon saké
½ cup mirin
½ cup shoyu

Place the water and kelp in a saucepan and let stand for 15 minutes. Cook over low heat and remove the kelp just before the water comes to a boil. Add the bonito flakes and cook over medium heat for 7 minutes. Add the seasonings and bring to a boil again. Strain through a strainer lined with a cheesecloth. Cool before serving.

Note: The sauce can be prepared beforehand and refrigerated.

Condiments:
　10 cm/4 inch length *daikon* radish, peeled, grated and drained in a colander
　3 green onions, finely chopped
　2–3 teaspoons grated *wasabi* horseradish

Tempura:
Vegetable oil for deep-frying
1 egg
Cold water to add to egg

Continued on page 124.

Udon Noodles with Beef Topping

(Niku-udon)

Udon soup, like *soba*, is usually served with a variety of toppings, although some *udon* connoisseurs say that the noodles can best be appreciated plain, with the soup alone. There are all kinds of traditional *udon* toppings, but I decided to introduce here a dish called *niku-udon,* which was a favorite of one of our American friends in Tokyo.

4 servings
Soup:
  6 cups *dashi* stock, see page 129
  2 teaspoons salt
  1 tablespoon shoyu
  1 tablespoon mirin
Topping:
  300 g/⅔ lb thinly sliced beef shoulder, cut into bite-sized pieces
  4 green onions, cut into 4 cm/½ inch lengths

  4 tablespoons saké
  2 tablespoons shoyu
  Dash of Japanese pepper powder
    (kona-zansho)
Seven spices (*shichimi togarashi*)
400 g/14 oz dried *udon* (wheat flour) noodles
4 cups boiling water to cook the noodles

1 Place the ingredients for the soup in a pot and bring to a boil.
2 Place the ingredients for the topping, except for the pepper and spices, in a shallow pan, and cook over medium heat until done, stirring frequently. Sprinkle with pepper.
3 Boil 4 cups of water in a big pot, add the noodles separately (see picture above) and stir until they again come to a boil. Cook the noodles al dente, checking by sampling a noodle or two for firmness. Drain the noodles in a colander and rinse them well in running water to remove excess starch, then drain again.
4 Dip the noodles in boiling water to reheat them, drain in a colander, and divide into 4 warmed noodle bowls (*domburi*) or deep soup bowls.
5 Pour the soup over the noodles and top with the topping. Serve immediately, accompanied by Japanese "seven spice" pepper to sprinkle on top at the table.

Note: If already cooked *udon* is used, omit step 3 but follow the other steps.

Rice Topped with Breaded Deep-Fried Pork

(Katsudon)

This seems to be one of the most popular *domburi* dishes—bowls of rice topped with other foods—among Westerners.

4 servings
4 fillets, 80 g/3 oz each, pork loin
Salt and pepper to taste
Flour to dredge pork
1 egg, beaten
Bread crumbs to coat pork
Vegetable oil for deep-frying
Cooking Liquid:
  2 cups *dashi* stock, see page 129
  5 tablespoons light-colored shoyu
  2 tablespoons mirin
1 onion, sliced
4 eggs, beaten separately
1 bunch *mitsuba* trefoil, cut into 3 cm/1 inch
  lengths
4 cups freshly boiled rice

1 Cut any threads along the sides of the pork fillets in a few places to prevent the meat from curling when cooked. Shake salt and pepper on both sides of the meat and dredge with flour. Dip in a beaten egg and coat with bread crumbs.

2 Heat oil in a deep-fryer to 180°C/365°F and deep-fry the breaded pork fillets until golden brown, turning a few times. Drain off the oil and cut into 2.5 cm/1 inch wide strips.

3 Mix the ingredients for the cooking liquid.

4 In a small shallow pan, place ¼ of the cooking liquid and onion slices and cook until the onion is soft. Add 1 portion of the fried pork cutlet in one layer, slowly pour in 1 beaten egg, and place ¼ of the *mitsuba* on top. Cover the pan, reduce the heat to low and simmer for 2 minutes, or until the egg has almost set.

5 Place 1 cup of rice in a *domburi* bowl, top with the pork and egg and serve. Repeat with the remaining ingredients.

Note: If you want to serve all the people at the same time, it may be quicker to use a larger pan to cook all the ingredients for the topping at one time and divide into 4 portions.

Sushi in Tofu Pouches

(*Inari-zushi*)

6–8 servings
6 cups freshly boiled rice, see page 75
Seasoned Vinegar:
  4 tablespoons rice vinegar
  4 tablespoons sugar
  2 teaspoons salt
Tofu pouches:
  30 sheets thin-fried tofu (*aburage*)
  3 cups boiling water
  ½ cup saké
  ½ cup shoyu
  ½ cup sugar
  3 tablespoons mirin
Pouch Filling:
  Vinegared rice from Step 1
  1 small burdock
  1 small carrot, peeled and finely chopped
  Cooking liquid from the thin-fried tofu
  Sweet pickled ginger (*amazu shoga*), sliced

1 Place freshly boiled rice in a large mixing bowl, (preferably a wooden bowl). Mix the ingredients for the seasoned vinegar and stir until the sugar and salt dissolve. Sprinkle over the rice and mix quickly, fanning with a hand-held fan so excess moisture evaporates.
2 Place the thin-fried tofu in one layer in a colander and pour boiling water over them to remove excess oil. Turn them over and repeat on the other side.
3 Boil the seasonings for the tofu pouches in a flat pan, add the fried tofu and cover with a drop lid. Cook over medium low heat for 12 minutes until a small amount of liquid remains. Remove the fried tofu and drain on a plate, returning the drained liquid to the pan.
4 Wash dirt from the burdock, scrape the skin with the back of a knife, and pare off shavings with a knife, as though you were sharpening a pencil. Dip shavings in cold water and leave until the water turns brown, then rinse under running water and drain. Add the burdock and carrots to the cooking liquid in the pan and cook until soft over low heat.
5 Mix the rice and vegetables and shape into 30 small rice balls. Fill the tofu pouches with the rice balls, and wrap them neatly. Serve with sweet pickled ginger.

Shoyu-Flavored Grilled Rice Balls

(*Yaki-Onigiri*)

Many Japanese who like to drink saké, especially older men, like to snack on a series of small servings of different foods as they drink. Before they leave the bar, however, they often ask for a rice dish, and these rice balls are among their favorites on such an occasion. This is also a tasty dish to bring along on a picnic.

4 servings
4 cups leftover boiled rice
Shoyu to baste
Pickles for garnish
1 Japanese cucumber, partially skinned
  and sliced

1 Form the rice into 8 triangular rice balls. To form a rice ball, first wet your hands and place ½ cup of rice on one palm. Encircle the rice with your fingers and grip it tightly, then alternate with each hand, pressing firmly until you have formed a triangular shape. Make seven more triangular balls in the same manner.
2 Grill both sides of the rice balls on a Japanese grill, which is set atop the burner on a stove. Baste the balls thoroughly with shoyu, using a basting brush, and grill again until nicely browned.
3 Serve with the cucumber, if desired.

Note: If a Japanese grill is not available, place the rice balls upright in an oven or toaster oven and bake them at 250°C/500°F for 10 minutes, then baste with shoyu. Bake a few more minutes to dry.

DESSERTS

Tofu Cake

Until quite recently nobody might have thought about making a dessert using tofu. Thanks to the globalization of cuisines, Japan has adopted not just foods but cooking ideas, methods and techniques from other counties, as well. This original recipe features tofu in a cheesecake-like dessert.

A 20 cm/8 inch layer cake, 4 servings
1 cake hard tofu (*momen-dofu*), drained and
  wrapped in paper towels (Picture 1)
3 egg yolks
3 tablespoons granulated sugar
Pinch of salt
5 tablespoons cornstarch
1 tablespoon lemon juice
½ teaspoon grated lemon rind
½ teaspoon vanilla extract
3 tablespoons fresh cream
2 tablespoons Cointreau (optional)
3 egg whites
3 tablespoons granulated sugar
4 sprigs of mint leaves for garnish

1 Preheat the oven to 180°C/ 375°F and line a 20 cm/8 inch layer cake tin with baking paper.   (Picture 1)
2 In a mixing bowl place the tofu and mix well with an electric mixer until smooth. Add the egg yolks, 3 tablespoons sugar, salt, cornstarch, lemon juice, lemon rind, vanilla and cream and blend until all the ingredients are evenly blended. Stir in the Cointreau.   (Picture 2)
3 In another mixing bowl, beat the egg whites until stiff, add the sugar, and keep beat-ing until silky. Fold the egg whites into the tofu mixture and pour into the prepared tin.
(Pictures 3–4)
4 Bake in the oven for 25–30 minutes, then leave in the oven until cool.
5 Garnish with mint leaves, if desired.

Persimmon Tart

(Kaki no Taruto)

For a 30 x 22 x 3 cm/12 x 8 x 1¹/4 inch pie pan

6 servings
Dough:
  1 cup sifted flour
  Pinch of salt
  5 tablespoons butter
  ½ cup sugar
  1 large egg, beaten
  Grated rind of 1 lemon
  100 g/4 oz powdered almond, toasted
  3 tablespoons sugar
Filling:
  3 persimmons, pared and sliced
    (Picture above)
  3 tablespoons sugar
  ½ cup water
  1 tablespoon Cointreau
Glaze:
  3 tablespoons apricot jam
  3 tablespoons sugar
  1 tablespoon Cointreau
1 cup whipped cream

1 Combine the flour, salt and butter in a mixing bowl, and cut the butter into small pieces, using a fork. Mix in the sugar and egg until smooth, and let stand for 30 minutes in the refrigerator.
2 Preheat the oven to 180°C/375°F.
3 Cook the persimmon in water and sugar until soft. Add the Cointreau and cool.
4 Place the dough on a greased pie pan and spread it with your fingers to line the bottom and side of the pan evenly.
5 Mix the almond powder and sugar and spread it evenly over the dough. Arrange the drained persimmons atop the powder, and bake in the oven for 30 minutes.
6 Cook the apricot jam, sugar and Cointreau, stirring constantly until it is bubbly and thick. Spoon the glaze over the persimmons. Serve with whipped cream.

Tofu Custard Pudding

4 servings
Butter to grease 4 oven-proof custard cups
3 tablespoons granulated sugar
1 tablespoon water
1 teaspoon shoyu
1 cake soft tofu (*kinugoshi-dofu*), drained with
  paper towels and cut into several pieces
1 egg
Pinch of salt
3 tablespoons granulated sugar
½ cup milk
¼ teaspoon vanilla extract

1 Place a baking pan half-filled with water in an oven. Preheat the oven to 170°C/350°F.
2 Grease with butter 4 custard cups.
3 In an empty skillet, cook the sugar and water over high heat until lightly browned. Add the shoyu and quickly pour the mixture into the custard cups.
4 In a food processor, mix tofu, egg, salt, sugar, milk and vanilla extract to a smooth consistency and pour into the custard cups.
5 Bake in the oven for 18 minutes. Chill until serving time.
6 Unmold upside-down in individual dessert bowls to serve.

Red and White Plum Blossoms

(Nishoku Baika-kan)

8–10 servings
2 sticks agar-agar, soaked until soft in cold
   water (see picture 1)
Red Blossoms:
   1 cooking apple, pared, cored and sliced
   3 tablespoons water to cook the apple
   1⅔ cups cold water
   5 tablespoons sugar
   Red artificial food coloring
   1 teaspoon cold water to dissolve the food
     coloring
White Blossoms:
   ¾ cup cold water
   5 tablespoons sugar
   1 cup milk
   5-6 drops almond extract

1 Squeeze the water from the agar-agar.
2 Cook the apple for the red blossoms in 3
tablespoons water until soft and purée in a
food processor or by putting through a fine sieve.
3 Break 1 stick of the agar-agar for the red blossoms into pieces and place in a pan with cold
water. Bring to a boil and cook slowly until the
agar-agar has completely melted.   (Picture 2)
4 Add sugar to the agar liquid and boil until
dissolved. Turn off the heat and pour the agar-
agar liquid bit by bit into the apple mixture, stirring for a smooth consistency.
5 Dilute the food coloring
with 1 teaspoon of water and
stir in the agar-agar mixture.
Pour into a wet, shallow pan to
set. Chill until serving.
6 Break the other stick of
agar-agar for the white blossom into pieces and cook in
water as in step 3.
7 Add the sugar and boil until
dissolved. Turn off the heat

and stir in milk and almond extract. Pour into a
wet, shallow pan to set. Chill until serving.
(Picture 3)
8 Cut the agar-agar of both colors with a
flower-shaped vegetable cutter or cookie cutter.
Lay one white blossom atop a red one to make
10 pairs and red blossoms atop white ones for
another 10 pairs, then serve.   (Picture 4)

Japanese Pear Sherbet

(Nashi no Shabetto)

15 servings
⅔ cup granulated sugar
⅔ cup water
2 large Japanese pears, pared and quartered
Juice from ½ lemon
3 tablespoons Cointreau
⅔ cup whipping cream, whipped to form
   soft peaks
Kiwi Fruit Sauce:
   5 kiwi fruit, peeled
   2 tablespoons granulated sugar
4 sprigs of mint leaves for garnish

1 Boil the sugar and water until the sugar dissolves, then chill.
2 Place the pears, syrup, lemon juice and Cointreau in a blender, and blend until smooth. Pour into a metal mixing bowl and freeze until half frozen or to the consistency of shaved ice.
3 Beat the sherbet with a whisk. Mix whipped cream into the sherbet and freeze until set.
4 Place the kiwi fruit, sugar and Cointreau in a blender, and blend until smooth. Chill.
5 Scoop sherbet into dessert bowls, pour the kiwi fruit sauce around each scoop, and serve.

Baked Figs

(Yaki-Ichijiku)

6 servings
6 large, ripe figs
3 tablespoons rum raisins (raisins soaked in rum for 1 week)
3 tablespoons granulated sugar
⅓ cup water
1 cinnamon stick
3 tablespoons rum
½ cup fresh cream
1 tablespoon granulated sugar
6 sprigs of mint leaves

1 Preheat an oven to 150°C/300°F.
2 Trim the stems from the figs and place the figs stem-side down in a pyrex or oven-proof ceramic baking dish.
3 Fill the hollows on top of the figs with rum raisins and sprinkle with sugar. Pour water in the baking dish and add the cinnamon stick.
4 Bake in the oven for 80 minutes or until figs are soft, pouring the cooking syrup over the figs several times while baking. Sprinkle remaining sugar, if any, over the figs.
5 Remove the dish from the oven, sprinkle rum over each fig and cool. Chill in a refrigerator overnight or until the sauce in the dish has thickened.
6 Whip the cream and sugar until they form soft peaks and spoon over the top of each fig before serving.
7 Place the baked figs in individual dessert dishes and top with whipped cream. Garnish with mint leaves.

Stewed Apples with Ice Cream

(Ringo no Ama-ni Aisukurimu-zoe)

4 servings
4 cooking apples (*kogyoku*), quartered and cored
6 tablespoons granulated sugar
4 tablespoons water
4 scoops vanilla ice cream
4 rounded tablespoons slivered almond slices, toasted

1 In a pot, place apples, sugar and water. Cook over medium heat until the apples are soft and all the liquid is absorbed. Reduce the heat gradually while cooking as the liquid decreases. Cool and chill until serving.
2 To serve, place apples in individual dessert bowls and scoop ice cream on top. Sprinkle almond slices over the ice cream and serve.

Menus for the Seasons

Spring

Vegetable Chips
(Yasai Sembei)

Clear Soup with Chicken Balls and *Enoki* Mushrooms
(Tori Dango to Enoki no Osumashi)

Hand-Rolled *Sushi*
(Temaki-zushi)

Fluffy Jelly with Strawberries
(Awayuki kan)

Vegetable Chips

(*Yasai Sembei*)

10 servings

2 small stalks lotus root
1 sweet potato
¼ Japanese pumpkin, seeded and
  thinly sliced
1 carrot, peeled and thinly sliced
½ small bunch dried Japanese
  angel-hair noodles, cut into
  5 cm/2 inch lengths
1 sheet, 20 cm/8-inch-square toasted
  dried *nori* laver, cut into strips
  1 x 5 cm/½ x 2 inch in length
Vegetable oil for deep-frying
Pinch of salt

1 Skin the lotus root and slice thinly. Dip it in cold water as you slice to remove excess starch and bitterness. Drain and shake dry.
2 Slice the sweet potato thinly and dip it in cold water to remove excess starch and bitterness. Drain and shake dry.
3 Pick up 4–5 pieces of the angel-hair noodles and wrap around one end a strip of dried *nori* laver slightly moistened with cold water. They are supposed to resemble pine leaves.
4 In a deep frying pan, heat oil to 170°C/350°F and deep-fry each vegetable and noodle bunch separately until crispy. Drain on a rack or atop paper towels. Sprinkle each vegetable and bunch of noodles with a pinch of salt to taste.

Note: You may wish to make this dish in advance and store it in a dry container.

Clear Soup with Chicken Balls and *Enoki* Mushrooms

(*Tori Dango to Enoki no Osumashi*)

10 servings
Meatballs:
  300 g/10 oz lean ground chicken
  ½ teaspoon salt
  1½ tablespoons saké
  2 teaspoons fresh ginger juice
  1½ tablespoons Japanese potato starch
    (*katakuri-ko*)
200 g/8 oz *enoki* mushrooms, roots removed
Pinch of salt
Clear Soup:
  8 cups *dashi* stock, see page 129
  2½ teaspoons salt
  2½ teaspoons light-colored shoyu
2 okra pods, thinly sliced

1 In a mixing bowl, combine the ground chicken and salt and mix well until they become slightly sticky. Add the saké, ginger juice, and starch and mix well again. Make the mixture into 20 meatballs by rolling in your palms.
2 In salted, boiling water, boil the *enoki* mushrooms for 1 minute and drain well. In the same pot, boil the meatballs until they rise to the top of the pot.
3 Divide the mushrooms and meatballs into 10

Hand-Rolled *Sushi*

(*Temaki-zushi*)

Hand-rolled *sushi* is becoming increasingly popular in *sushi* bars. I have often served it at home, with great success. My friends love it, as they are able to include whatever ingredients they like and to eat as much as they want.

10 servings
Sushi rice:
  6 cups Japanese rice
  6 cups water
  1 piece, 20 cm/8 inch length dried kelp
    (*dashi-kombu*) for *dashi* stock
  3 tablespoons saké

Vinegar Mixture:
  ½ cup and 2 tablespoons Japanese rice
    vinegar
  2 tablespoons sugar
  1 tablespoon salt

Ingredients to be rolled:

200 g/½ lb block of tuna for *sushi*, cut into sticks the size of French-fried potatoes

200 g/½ lb block of squid or cuttlefish for *sushi*, cut into narrow 5 cm/ 2 inch lengths

10 fresh sweet shrimp, shelled and deveined

½ cup salted salmon roe

5 cm/½ inch piece of yellow pickled radish (*takuan*), thinly sliced and shredded

10 green *shiso* leaves

1 Japanese cucumber, cut into 5 cm/2 inch long sticks or 10 miniature cucumbers

8 stalks pickled wild burdock (*yama-gobo*), cur into 5 cm/2 inch lengths

100 g/½ lb sweet pink pickled ginger slices

30 sheets, 20 x 20 cm/8 x 8-inch, of toasted *nori* laver, cut in halves

1 fresh Japanese *wasabi* horseradish, skin scraped or use 3 tablespoons prepared grated *wasabi*, or 2 tablespoons powdered *wasabi* mixed with 1 tablespoon cold water

Shoyu for dipping

1 Wash the rice and soak in an equal amount of water together with the kelp and saké for 30 minutes. Start to cook over medium heat. When the steam begins to rise after about 12 minutes, uncover and remove the kelp. Cover again and raise the heat to very high. Reduce heat just before it boils over, and simmer for 20 minutes. Raise the heat again to very high to evaporate all the liquid. Turn off the heat, and insert a paper towel or cooking towel between the pan and the lid. Let it stand for 5 minutes.

2 Stir the ingredients for the vinegar mixture until the sugar and salt are dissolved. Place the rice in a large mixing bowl (a wooden one is ideal if available), sprinkle the vinegar dressing over the rice and toss thoroughly, quickly fanning the rice to remove excess moisture. Cover the rice bowl with a damp towel to prevent the rice from drying. Place in a serving bowl.

3 Arrange the seafood, pickled radish, *shiso* leaves, cucumber, pickled burdock, *wasabi* horseradish and ginger on a platter. Serve the toasted laver in a separate dry container. Prepare small individual serving dishes containing 2 teaspoons shoyu.

4 To eat: Spread rice thinly atop a sheet of *nori* laver, covering half of it and leaving space on both sides. Place a small dollop of green horseradish in the center of the rice followed by ingredients of your choice. Roll up from the side which is spread with rice. Dip the *sushi* occa-

sionally in soy sauce and try slices of pickled ginger to refresh your palate.

Note: You can use any other ingredients you may have seen at a *sushi* bar or that may strike your fancy. Cheese, ham cut in sticks, and Vienna sausage pleased the children at a party I gave for my sons.

Fluffy Jelly with Strawberries

(Awayuki-kan)

1 stick agar-agar, softened in cold water for 20 minutes

1 cup cold water

1 cup granulated sugar

1 cup milk

2 egg whites, stiffly beaten

½ teaspoon almond extract (optional)

15 large strawberries, hulled and halved lengthwise

1 Break softened agar-agar into small pieces and place in a pan with cold water. Bring to a boil and simmer until the agar-agar melts, skimming off the bubbles on top.

2 Add sugar and cook, stirring, until the sugar dissolves. Strain through a strainer lined with a cheesecloth.

3 Stir the agar-agar mixture gradually into the beaten egg whites and mix in the strawberries.

4 Transfer the mixture into a 4–5 cup gelatine mold and cool or chill to set. Cut into serving portions with a sharp knife before serving.

Summer

Fried Seafood and Vegetables on
the Skewer
(*Kushi-age*)

Miso Soup with Turnips and
Thin-Fried Tofu
(*Kabu to Aburage no Miso-shiru*)

Tofu and Spinach Salad
(*Tofu to Horenso no Wafu Sarada*)

Mushroom Rice
(*Kinoko Gohan*)

Adzuki Bean Paste and Fresh
Fruit in Dark Syrup
(*Furutsu Anmitsu*)

Fried Seafood and Vegetables on the Skewer

(Kushi-age)

10 servings
20 shrimp, shelled and deveined
10 fresh scallops
240 g/8 oz salmon fillet, skinned and cut
  into bite-sized pieces
Salt and pepper to taste
240 g/8 oz preferred type of cheese,
  cut into 10 slices
100 bamboo skewers
100 g/4 oz ground chicken
1 teaspoon fresh ginger juice
2 teaspoons saké
2 teaspoons cornstarch
1 small stalk lotus root, peeled
10 button mushrooms
10 baby onions, peeled and parboiled
10 Brussels sprouts, parboiled
30 fresh gingko nuts, shelled and skinned
Flour for dredging
2–3 eggs, beaten
Bread crumbs for coating
Vegetable oil for deep-frying
1 lemon, cut in half and sliced
Dipping Sauce A:
  200 g/8 oz daikon radish, skinned, grated
    and drained in a colander
  4 tablespoons chopped chives (asatsuki)
  4 tablespoons Japanese rice vinegar
  6 tablespoons shoyu
  3 tablespoons mirin
  3 tablespoons dashi stock, see page 129
Dipping Sauce B:
  ¾ cup tomato ketchup
  1 tablespoon prepared hot mustard
  4 tablespoons Worcestershire sauce

1 Sprinkle shrimp, scallops and salmon with salt and pepper. Skewer each piece of the seafood and cheese separately with bamboo skewers.
2 Mix well ground chicken, ginger juice, saké and cornstarch and stuff the holes of the lotus root. Slice the stuffed lotus into 8 mm/⅓ inch thick pieces.
3 Skewer one piece each of the lotus root, mushrooms, onions, and Brussels sprouts on one bamboo skewer, together with 3 gingko nuts.
4 Dredge all the skewered ingredients with flour, dip them in beaten eggs and coat with bread crumbs. Arrange them on a serving platter.
5 Mix separately the ingredients for Dipping Sauces A and B and pour into sauce boats separately.
6 Prepare a heating unit on the table and heat oil in a deep frying pan atop it to 170°C/360°F. Have each diner pick up a skewer with their favorite foods and dip it in the oil to fry until golden brown. He or she then dips the food either in Sauce A or B, or sprinkles it with lemon juice to eat.

Miso Soup with Turnips and Thin-Fried Tofu

(Kabu to Aburage no Miso-shiru)

10 servings
8 cups dashi stock, see page 129
5 small white turnips, skinned and quartered
  lengthwise
2 sheets thin-fried tofu (aburage), shredded
3 turnip leaves, chopped
5 tablespoons dark miso paste

1 In a soup pan, place the dashi stock and turnips and cook until the turnips are softened.
2 Pour boiling water over the thin-fried tofu in a colander and drain. Add to the soup together with the turnip leaves.
3 Place the miso paste in a soup ladle and dilute it with some stock from the pan. Add to the soup and serve immediately.

Tofu and Spinach Salad

(Tofu to Horenso no Wafu Sarada)

This is my new favorite tofu recipe. Draining the tofu thoroughly by wrapping it in several layers of paper towels is the key to its success.

10 servings
450 g/1 lb spinach leaves
1 bunch daikon sprouts, roots removed
20 green shiso leaves, shredded
20 fresh button mushrooms, thinly sliced

2 large tomatoes, cut into bite-sized pieces
2 cakes soft tofu (*kinugoshi-dofu*), drained
  and diced
5 bacon slices, cooked until crisp and torn
  into small bits
Shoyu-Vinegar Dressing:
  2 teaspoons sugar
  4 tablespoons shoyu
  4 tablespoons Japanese rice vinegar
  2 tablespoons mirin
  1 tablespoon sesame oil
  6 tablespoons salad oil
  1 tablespoon grated fresh ginger root

1 Dip spinach leaves, *daikon* sprouts and *shiso* leaves in ice water for added crispness. Drain them in a colander and shake well to dry.
2 Mix the vegetables with mushrooms and tomatoes and place them in a salad bowl. Place the tofu atop the vegetables and sprinkle with bacon bits.
3 Mix the ingredients for the dressing and pour it over the salad right before serving.

Mushroom Rice

(Kinoko Gohan)

10 servings
4 cups Japanese rice, rinsed and drained
4 cups *dashi* stock, see page 129,
  cooled to room temperature
240 g/8 oz fresh *shiitake* mushrooms,
  quartered, with stem tips trimmed off
240 g/8 oz *shimeji* mushrooms, stems
  separated and roots cut off
240 g/8 oz. *maitake* mushrooms, cut into
  small pieces
4 tablespoons shoyu
3 tablespoons saké
3 sheets thin-fried tofu (*aburage*),
  cut into small pieces
¾ teaspoon salt

1 Place the rice and the stock in a thick pan, and let stand for 30 minutes.
2 Place all the mushrooms in a mixing bowl and sprinkle with shoyu and saké. Let stand for 10 minutes.
3 Add the mushrooms and the sauce to the rice. Add fried tofu and salt and stir lightly.

4 Cook the rice over low-medium heat until it comes to a boil. Raise the heat to high and cook for 2 minutes. Reduce the heat to low and simmer for 20 minutes. Raise the heat to high again for 10 seconds and turn it off. Insert one sheet of cooking paper or paper towel between the pan and the lid and let stand for 20 minutes before serving.

Adzuki Bean Paste and Fresh Fruit in Dark Syrup

(Furutsu Anmitsu)

10 servings
Dark Syrup:
  1 cup water
  1 cup sugar
  1 cup dark brown rock sugar
  1 tablespoon liquid candy, see page 137) or
    heavy corn syrup
1 stick agar-agar, see page 117
2 cups cold water
¾ cup glutinous rice flour, see page 122
¼ cup sugar
¼ cup cold water
1½ cups canned boiled adzuki beans
10 large fresh strawberries, hulled
1 honeydew melon, diced
3 medium bananas, according to sizes, sliced

1 Bring the ingredients for the dark syrup to a boil and continue boiling over medium heat for 10 minutes. Cool to room temperature.
2 Soak the agar-agar stick in cold water for 10 minutes to soften. Squeeze dry and break into small pieces. Place in a pan with 2 cups of cold water and cook to dissolve completely. Pour the agar-agar liquid into a square pan and cool to room temperature to set. Cut into small pieces.
3 In a mixing bowl, mix well the glutinous rice flour, ¼ cup sugar and ¼ cup cold water, until it forms a smooth paste. Form 20 small balls by rolling them in your palms, and pinch each one lightly between your thumb and index finger to flatten. Cook the dumplings in boiling water until they float to the top. Drain them and dip in ice water to cool. Drain well in a colander.
4 In individual serving dessert bowls, divide the agar-agar, adzuki bean paste, dumplings and fruit. Pour the syrup over the ingredients and serve.

Fall

Party Lunch Box
(*Shokado Bento*)

Clear Soup with Sea Clams
(*Hamaguri no Ushio-jiru*)

Sweet Potatoes à la Mont Blanc
(*Satsuma-imo no Monburan*)

Tomato Salad with *Shiso* Leaves
(*Tomato Sarada Ao-jiso Fumi*)

Party Lunch Box

(Shokado Bento)

10 servings
Molded Rice
8 cups freshly boiled rice
10 salted cherry blossoms (*sakura no shio-zuke*)

Divide the rice into 10 portions and place in molds. Remove from the molds and place in the front, left compartment of each *bento* (lunch) box. Place 1 salted cherry blossom atop each serving of molded rice.

Chicken Teriyaki
2 chicken breasts
3 tablespoons sugar
5 tablespoons shoyu
3 tablespoons mirin

1 Mix well the chicken, sugar, shoyu and mirin in a mixing bowl and let stand for 10 minutes.
2 Heat an oven to 180°C/375°F.
3 Place the chicken in one layer in a baking pan and bake in the oven for 25 minutes. Slice each chicken breast into 1.3 cm/½ inch thick pieces.

Spicy Lotus Root
2 stalks lotus root, skinned and
  thinly sliced
3 tablespoons sugar
1 teaspoon salt
½ cup Japanese rice vinegar
¼ cup cold water
2 dried red chili peppers, seeded
  and chopped

1 Dip the lotus root in cold water as you slice them to remove excess starch.
2 Put the lotus in boiling water and cook until the water boils again.
3 In a mixing bowl, mix well the sugar, salt, rice vinegar and water until the sugar and salt dissolve. Add the lotus root and chili peppers and let sit for 30 minutes. Drain before serving.

Tied Fish Cake
2 small pink fish cakes on wooden boards,
  sliced thinly in 20 pieces

1 Slice each piece of the fish cake down the center, leaving both ends uncut.
2 Slice the piece again from the left end parallel to the first slice, leaving the right end uncut. Do the same to the right side of the central slit from the opposite direction.
3 Insert one cut end through the central slit from one side and the other cut end from the other side so that they appear to have been tied. Do the same to the other slices.

Place the Chicken Teriyaki, Spicy Lotus Root and Tied Fish Cake in the front, right compartment of each *bento* box.

Sashimi
2 fresh fillets (200 g/14 oz. each)
  whitemeat fish such as red snapper,
  turbot, young yellowtail (*hamachi*)
10 green *shiso* leaves
2 packages *daikon* sprouts, roots cut off
Grated Japanese *wasabi* horseradish
Shoyu for dipping fish

Slice thinly the fish fillets and place 3 slices together with the *shiso* leaves, *daikon* sprouts, and *wasabi* horseradish in the section of the *bento* box which is on your right and farthest from you when served.

Steamed Shrimp
20 shrimp, deveined
½ teaspoon salt
3 tablespoons saké

1 In a shallow pan, place shrimp and sprinkle with salt and saké.
2 Cover the pan and cook the shrimp quickly over high heat just until they turn red.
3 Cool and shell them, but leave their tails on.

Simmered Vegetables
4 carrots, peeled and cut into
  30 flower-shaped pieces
3 cups *dashi* stock, see page 129
3 tablespoons sugar
1½ teaspoons salt
3 tablespoons light-colored shoyu
4 tablespoons mirin
30 fresh *shiitake* mushrooms, stemmed
20 fresh green beans, cut into 3 cm/1¼ inch
  lengths, parboiled

1 Cook the carrots until mostly soft in the stock.

2 Add the *shiitake* mushrooms, sugar, salt, shoyu and mirin and cook for 5 minutes longer.
3 Add the green beans and cook for 1 more minute.

Arrange the shrimp and simmered vegetables in the last empty compartment of each *bento* box.

Clear Soup with Sea Clams

(Hamaguri no Ushio-jiru)

Ushio in Japanese means "sea water," and *Ushio-jiru* means "sea water soup." This name is given to a clear soup made with fish or shellfish. This particular soup with sea clams is made on Girls' Day, or the Doll Festival on March 3rd. On this day, many families with girls display a set of traditional Japanese dolls and celebrate with mixed vegetable sushi *(gomoku-zushi)*, sweet white rice wine *(ama-zake)*, a set of tricolor diamond-shaped rice cakes *(hishi-mochi)* and this soup.

2 pieces, 10 x 10 cm/4 x 4 inch dried kelp
  (dashi-kombu)
8 cups cold water
20 large sea clams *(hamaguri)*
2 teaspoons salt
2 tablespoons saké
2 teaspoons shoyu
10 young leaves of *kinomé*

1 Place the kelp and water in a soup pan and let stand for 15 minutes.
2 Clean the clam shells with a brush. Most clams on the market have already had the sand removed before they are sold; if not, dip them in 3% salt water for a few hours to allow the clams to spit out the sand.
3 Bring the kelp and water slowly to a boil over medium-low heat. Remove the kelp before the water begins to boil. Raise the heat to high.
4 Add the clams and cook until the shells open. Turn off the heat and remove the clams from the pan. Using the tip of a small knife, gently separate half of the clams from their shells. Place the other clams, still in their shells, in ten lacquered soup bowls, one per bowl. Then place an already separated clam in the empty half of each shell.

5 Season the soup with salt, saké and shoyu. Bring to a boil and pour into the bowls. Top with *kinome* leaves and serve.

Sweet Potatoes à la Mont Blanc

(Satsuma imo no Monburan)

This is a very popular cake, especially among girls young and old in Japan, and you can find it at almost any cake shop. But you can make it too, substituting sweet potatoes for chestnuts. Good fresh chestnuts are available only in fall, but good sweet potatoes are available almost all year round.

10 servings
900 g/2 lb sweet potatoes, peeled and
  sliced into 3 mm/$1/8$ inch thick pieces
6 tablespoons butter
20 sweet chestnuts in syrup from the jar,
  syrup reserved
1 cup sugar
$3/4$ teaspoon salt
$1/2$ cup fresh cream
$1/2$ teaspoon vanilla extract
2 tablespoons brandy
1 cup fresh cream
1 tablespoon sugar

1 Rinse the potatoes in cold water to remove the starch, continuing to rinse until the water runs clear.
2 Cook the potatoes until soft in just enough water to cover.
3 Mash, or put the potatoes through a fine sieve while hot. Add butter, chestnuts with syrup, sugar, salt and $1/2$ cup cream. Cook 3–4 minutes over medium heat, stirring constantly. Add flavorings (vanilla and brandy) and cool.
4 Whip 1 cup of cream and the sugar until they form soft peaks on the whisk.
5 Scoop the potato mixture into individual serving dishes and serve with the whipped cream on top.

Tomato Salad with *Shiso* Leaves
(Tomato Sarada Ao-jiso Fumi)

Continued on page 111.

108

Winter

Crab Salad in Peach Halves
(*Kani no Mayonezu Pichi-zume*)

Spicy Marinated Chicken
(*Tori no Namban-zuke*)

Stuffed Mushrooms with Shrimp
(*Matsukasa-age*)

Pickled Plum Rice Balls
(*Ume-shiso O-musubi*)

***Mikan* Tangerine Cup Jelly**
(*Mikan Zeri*)

Crab Salad in Peach Halves

(Kani no Mayonezu Pichi-zume)

This is an ideal dish to start off any meal. It's quick and easy to prepare, and everyone who has tried it at our home has just loved it.

10 servings
250 g/9 oz canned crab meat, drained and
  with cartilage removed
Juice from 1 lemon
7 tablespoons mayonnaise
10 canned yellow peach halves, drained
Lettuce or chervil to garnish

1 Sprinkle the crab meat with lemon juice and set aside for a few minutes.
2 Mix the crab and mayonnaise. Fill the hollows of the peach halves with the crab mixture. Garnish with lettuce or chervil leaves and serve.

Spicy Marinated Chicken

(Tori no Namban-zuke)

10 servings
1 whole, 1.4 kg/3 lb chicken, cut up
4 tablespoons saké
6 tablespoons shoyu
3 tablespoons fresh ginger juice, see page 69
Japanese potato starch (*katakuri-ko*) or
  cornstarch for dredging the chicken
Vegetable oil for deep-frying
Marinade:
 1 leek, sliced
 5 slices fresh ginger root
 2 dried red chili peppers, seeded and chopped
 6 tablespoons sugar
 3 tablespoons saké
 7 tablespoons shoyu
 4 tablespoons Japanese rice vinegar
 2 tablespoons sesame oil
10 okra pods
Pinch of salt

1 In a mixing bowl, combine the chicken pieces, saké, shoyu and ginger juice and let stand for 30 minutes.

2 Dredge the chicken thoroughly in the potato starch.
3 Heat oil in a fryer to 170°C/350°F and deep-fry the chicken pieces until nicely browned. Drain off the oil and place the chicken in a large mixing bowl.
4 In a saucepan, bring the ingredients for the marinade to a boil and pour it over the fried chicken pieces. Marinate them for 30 minutes or longer, turning occasionally.
5 Boil the okras in salted boiling water until they turn bright green and drain.
6 Arrange the chicken and okras in a serving dish before serving.

Stuffed Mushrooms with Shrimp

(Matsukasa-age)

10 servings
30 fresh *shiitake* mushrooms, stems trimmed
  off and reserved
Japanese potato starch (*katakuri-ko*)
Filling Ingredients:
 300 g/¾ lb shrimp, shelled and deveined
 Stems of the *shiitake* mushrooms,
  finely chopped
 1 teaspoon salt
 2 teaspoons ginger juice, see page 69
 2 tablespoons *saké*
 2 teaspoon sugar
 1 egg white, beaten
 4 tablespoons Japanese potato starch
Bread crumbs for coating
Vegetable oil for deep-frying
Parsley for garnish

1 Chop the shrimp finely, until it becomes pasty, or make it into a paste using a food processor. Mix all the other ingredients for the filling.
2 Dredge the mushrooms caps in Japanese potato starch and stuff them with the filling, using a spoon or a table knife.
3 Coat the stuffed side of the mushrooms with bread crumbs.
4 Heat oil for deep-frying to 180°C/365°F and fry the stuffed mushrooms until nicely browned on the stuffed side, turning once. Drain off the oil.
5 Arrange the mushrooms on a serving platter

with some parsley.

Alternative:
Ground chicken or pork is a good substitute for shrimp.

Pickled Plum Rice Balls

(Ume-shiso Omusubi)

10 servings
10 cups freshly boiled rice
7 pickled Japanese plums *(umeboshi)*, cored
  and chopped
20 green *shiso* leaves, chopped

1 Mix the rice, pickled plums, and *shiso* leaves lightly and quickly.
2 Pour cold water into a mixing bowl.
3 Wet your hands with the water and place about ½ cup of the rice mixture in one of your palms. Make it into a ball, by gripping and rolling it in your hand. Do the same to the remaining rice to form 20 rice balls in all.

Note: If you are not successful in forming the rice into balls, you can use the plastic rice-ball molds in different shapes that are sold in Japanese-style food stores.

Mikan Tangerine Cup Jelly

(Mikan Zeri)

10 servings
2 tablespoons powdered gelatin
6 tablespoons white wine
10 *mikan* tangerines
4 tablespoons granulated sugar
3 tablespoons Cointreau or other orange liqueur

1 Dissolve the gelatin in wine.
2 Cut off the top ¼ portion of each *mikan* and remove the flesh to make 10 cups. Squeeze out the juice of the *mikan* flesh.
3 Add the sugar and Cointreau to the juice and mix well to dissolve the sugar.
4 Melt the dissolved gelatin in a double boiler

or microwave oven and stir into the juice.
5 Divide the liquid into the cups and chill in a refrigerator to set for 3–4 hours. Garnish with green leaves, if desired.

Continued from page 107.

Tomato Salad with *Shiso* Leaves

(Tomato Sarada Ao-jiso Fumi)

10 servings
4 lettuce leaves, torn into bite-sized pieces
10 medium-sized tomatoes, sliced 1 cm/
  ½ inch thick
20 green *shiso* leaves, chopped
Shoyu-Vinegar Dressing:
  2 teaspoons sugar
  4 tablespoons Japanese rice vinegar
  2 tablespoons shoyu
  6 tablespoons salad oil

1 Line a shallow salad bowl with lettuce, place tomatoes over it and top with *shiso* leaves. Chill until serving time.
2 Mix the ingredients for the dressing and chill. Pour the dressing over the salad just before serving.

Notes on Cooking Ingredients and Procedures

Cooking Ingredients

I. Dried Stock Ingredients

1. Dried kelp for stock (*Dashi-kombu*)
Wider, thicker kelp has richer flavor. White coating on surface is source of flavor, so do not wash before using.

2. Dried bonito fillets and fish flakes
Top, right of photo below: whole dried bonito fillet (*katsuo-bushi*). 1 fillet is 1/4 of entire bonito. Steamed, smoked and dried for months until it resembles a tree bark.
Top, left: thick bonito flakes (*katsuo no atsu-kezuri*). Thickly shaved fillet of dried bonito. Used for making strong soup stock and dipping sauce for buckwheat and white wheat flour noodles.
Middle: mixed fish flakes (*kongo-kezuribushi*). Mixes flakes from bonito, mackerel and sardines, so stock made with these flakes often has slight fish taste. Often used for cooking vegetables.
Low, right: regular bonito flakes (*hanagatsuo*). Flakes made solely from bonito. Used to make Number One stock. Brightly colored, large flakes are freshest.

3. Boiled and dried sardines (*niboshi*)
Young, whole, 5-cm/2-inch-long sardines are boiled and completely dried. Good for soybean paste (*miso*) soup with root vegetables or vegetable stew.

Top, right: whole dried bonito fillet
Top, left: thick bonito flakes Middle: mixed fish flakes
Bottom: regular bonito flakes

Dried kelp (*kombu*)

Dried sardines

II. Herbs and Spices

1. White raw sesame seeds (*shiro no arai-goma*)
Toasted, ground and used for Japanese salad dressings and dipping sauce for shabu-shabu.
Black raw sesame seeds (*kuro no arai-goma*)
Same flavor as white sesame seeds. Seldom used for salad dressings but toasted with salt and sprinkled over steamed red glutinous rice with adzuki beans.

2. Powdered Japanese pepper (*kona-zansho*)
Powdered Japanese dried pepper berries. Often used with beef dishes, grilled eel and other meat dishes. One of the "seven spices" (*shichimi*).

3. Japanese peppercorns (*mi-zansho*)
Japanese pepper trees bloom in early spring and berries ripen in early summer. Boiled, then preserved by being marinated in vinegar.

4. Japanese mustard (*wa-garashi*)
More pungent than Western mustard. Prepare by mixing thoroughly with boiling hot water, letting stand for one minute.

5. Wasabi horseradish (*wasabi*)
Grows only in cold, clean water in rocky streams. Essential for *sashimi* and *sushi* and for the dipping sauce for buckwheat noodles.

6. Grated wasabi horseradish in a tube (*oroshi-wasabi*)

Grated *wasabi* in a tube is convenient, more economical than fresh *wasabi*.

7. Ginger root (*shoga*)
Shredded and chopped for use in cooking fish and meat. Grated as condiment for chilled tofu, *sashimi* and other dishes. Juice from grated ginger is used in marinade for meat and fish.

8. Yuzu citrus (*yuzu*)
Rind is used for seasonal flavor for such dishes as *chawan-mushi*, *dobin-mushi*, clear soup. Juice is used in sauce for *nabemono*, marinade for fish, salad dressing.

9. Daidai citrus (*daidai*)
Placed atop rice cakes as New Year's decoration. Juice is used in dipping sauce for winter *nabemono*.

10. Sudachi citrus (*sudachi*)
Smallest citrus fruit in Japan, has dark-green skin. Juice is used in many foods and drinks in late summer and early autumn.

11. Kabosu citrus (*kabosu*)
Juice is used just like *sudachi*. Juicier than sudachi, but lacks its delicate flavor. Rind is not used.

12. Seven spices, ground (*shichimi-togarashi*)
Literally, a mix of seven spices. A typical mix in Tokyo includes baked and ground red peppers, dried and ground red peppers, Japanese *sansho* pepper, black sesame seeds, poppy seeds, hemp seeds and dried citrus peel. Ingredients may vary in other areas; could include such foods as dried green laver or perilla (*shiso*), or more than seven ingredients may be used.

13. Japanese chili pepper paste
(*yuzu-kosho, kanzuri*)
Hot pepper paste flavored with *yuzu* citrus. The paste is named *kanzuri* in the area where it originated and where it is most often used today.

14. Dried red chili pepper
(*aka-togarashi, taka no tsumé*)
2.5–5 cm/1–2-inch-long dried red peppers are the hottest spices used in Japanese cooking. Thin slices of the pepper are used in traditional dishes like *kimpira-gobo*.

15. Ginger flowers (*myoga*)
Buds of a plant of the ginger family. Sliced and served as condiments for chilled tofu and other dishes in summer.

Herbs and Spices

White and black raw sesame seeds

Powdered Japanese pepper (*kona-zansho*)

Japanese peppercorns (*mi-zansho*)

Japanese mustard (*wa-garashi*)

Wasabi horseradish (*wasabi*)

Grated wasabi horseradish in a tube

Ginger root (*shoga*)

Yuzu citrus (*yuzu*)

Sudachi citrus (*sudachi*)

Kabosu citrus (*kabosu*)

Seven spices (*shichimi-togarashi*)

Japanese chili pepper paste (*kanzuri*)

Dried red chili peppers
(*aka-togarashi, taka no tsumé*)

Ginger flowers (*myoga*)

Japanese pepper leaves (*kinomé*)

Green perilla (*shiso*) leaves (*ao-jiso*)

Perilla (*shiso*) flowers (*ho-jiso*)

Purple smartweed (*beni-tade*)

Hama-bofu (*hama-bofu*)

Daikon sprouts (*kaiware-na*)

Green onions (*banno-negi*)

Chives (*asatsuki*)

Mitsuba trefoil (*mitsuba*)

16. Japanese pepper leaves (*kinomé*)
Fresh young, light green leaves of *sansho* tree, used in season to prepare dishes with bamboo shoots.

17. Green perilla (*shiso*) leaves (*ao-jiso*)
One of the most popular herbs in Japan today. Is almost always used when *sashimi* or other uncooked dishes are served.

18. Perilla (*shiso*) flowers (*ho-jiso*)
The perilla plant puts forth tiny pink flowers in summer, which are served with *sashimi* as a garnish.

19. Purple smartweed (*beni-tade*)
Dark purple seed leaves of grass which grows by the river or marsh. Slightly pungent and aromatic. Often served with *sashimi*.

20. Hama-bofu (*hama-bofu*)
Small, aromatic twigs of a plant which grows on sandy beaches (*hama*). Served with *sashimi* as a condiment.

21. Daikon sprouts (*kaiware-na*)
These sprouts of the *daikon* plant have a slightly pungent taste similar to cress. Used in salads and with raw fish.

22. Green onions (*banno negi*)
Japanese soup dishes are often garnished with chopped green onion. *Banno negi* can be a substitute for most other types of onions in cooking.

23. Chives (*asatsuki*)
Chopped chives are often added to dipping sauce for *nabemono*.

24. Mitsuba trefoil (*mitsuba*)
A leaf vegetable featuring a long, thin stem topped with three attractive leaves. Its pleasant aroma makes it a popular addition to *nabemono* and a tasty topping for soups.

Fish and Shellfish

Sea bream (*tai*)

Gold-eyed red snapper (*kinme-dai*)

Horse mackerel (*aji*)

Smelt (*kisu*)

Tiger shrimp (*kuruma-ebi*)

Sweet red shrimp (*ama-ebi*)

Squid (*ika*)

Octopus (*tako*)

Large sea clams (*hamaguri*)

Small sea clams (*asari*)

Salted salmon roe (*ikura*)

Top: Baked fish cake (*yaki-ita*)
Bottom: Steamed fish cake (*kamaboko*)

Toasted nori laver (*yaki-nori*)

Wakamé kelp, dried (*wakamé*)

Dried agar-agar (*bo-kanten*)

III. Fish and Shellfish

1. Sea bream, red snapper (*tai*)
A highly regarded fish among Japanese, often served on birthdays and other festive occasions. Can be cooked in a variety of ways.

2. Gold-eyed red snapper (*kinme-dai*)
Best liked when boiled. Often used for *nabemono*.

3. Horse mackerel (*aji*)
Silver skinned whitemeat fish that is a very popular meal choice. Typically eaten broiled with salt or in sushi or chopped up for *sashimi*. Dried *aji* is also a commonly eaten breakfast food.

4. Smelt (*kisu*)
Light, soft whitemeat fish that lacks distinctive flavor, popular for use in tempura. It is often opened up flat when sold in the store.

5. Tiger shrimp (*kuruma-ebi*)
Always sold alive. When boiled it becomes clear red and white in color, with a sweet taste. Because of its festive red and white colors, it is often used to garnish dishes.

6. Sweet red shrimp (*ama-ebi*)
Small as one's little finger, these shrimp are always eaten fresh as sashimi or the topping for *sushi*.

7. Squid (*ika*)
Size varies from finger size to several feet. Skin is peeled from larger squid, but fish is never pounded. Served uncooked as *sashimi*, grilled or boiled.

8. Octopus (*tako*)
Octopus in the stores is almost always boiled, and the skin is a deep red. It is sliced fairly thin and served as *sashimi* or combined with cucumber slices in a vinegared salad.

9. Large sea clams (*hamaguri*)
Often cooked in clear soup, broiled in salt, or steamed in saké. Rarely eaten uncooked in Japan.

10. Small sea clams (*asari*)
Usually served in miso soup.

11. Salted salmon roe (*ikura*)
Served as topping for *sushi*. May also be preserved in saké or shoyu.

12. Fish cake (*kamaboko*)
Slices often served with *wasabi* as hors d'oeuvre.
Top in photo: baked fish cake (*yaki-ita*)
Fish meat paste mixed with grated taro potato and baked atop wooden sheet.
Bottom: steamed fish cake (*kamaboko*)
Fish cake which has been steamed instead of baked.

13. Nori laver, toasted (*yaki-nori*)
Made with seaweed fibers like hand-made paper. Used to wrap rolled and hand-rolled *sushi*. Crushed and sprinkled over noodles.

14. Wakamé kelp, dried (*wakamé*)
Thin, nearly black long seaweed that is dried. Soaked in cold water for 5 minutes before being used in salads and soups. Turns dark-green after being soaked.

15. Dried agar-agar (*bo-kanten*)
A vegetable gelatin that sets at room temperature. Often served with syrup and fruit as dessert.

IV. Vegetables and Nuts

1. Chrysanthemum leaves (*shungiku*)
Edible chrysanthemum leaves originally brought from the Mediterranean area several hundred years ago. Often used in shabu-shabu, *nabemono* and salads.

2. Komatsuna (*komatsu-na*)
A leaf vegetable of the brassica family available mainly in the Tokyo area. Resembles spinach but differs in color of the roots, texture and flavor. Is often stir-fried or cooked with fried tofu.

3. Leek (*naga-negi*)
Typically, only the white portion is eaten. It is often found in *nabemono* and *miso* soup. It is also chopped for use as a condiment for various noodles.

4. Spring onion (*wakegi*)
This soft, long green onion is mainly used for a salad called *nuta*, which is dressed with a *miso*-based dressing.

5. Japanese white radish (*daikon*)
Daikon is best in winter, although it is available all year round. It is usually grated, sliced into salad, pickled with salted rice bran, or boiled with octopus, fried tofu and other foods.

6. Small turnip (*ko-kabu*)
Best in winter and spring. Both the roots and the leaves are cooked with fried tofu. It is also tasty in miso soup and when pickled.

7. Burdock (*gobo*)
A long, dark-skinned and fibrous root vegetable that is good for the bowels. Often cooked in dishes like *tataki-gobo*, or salad with sesame dressing.

8. Lotus root (*renkon, hasu*)
Grown in muddy rice paddies. The root consists of several hollowed-out nodes. These have a crunchy texture that is best savored when stir-fried with chili pepper or cooked in a vinegared salad.

9. Bamboo shoots (*takenoko*)
Although bamboo shoots are available year round, spring is the season for fresh bamboo shoots. It is boiled during the other seasons. Often stewed with meat and other vegetables.

10. Sweet potato (*satsuma-imo*)
The best, and sweetest, sweet potatoes are of a golden yellow color inside. They are roasted, steamed and made into a variety of snacks and desserts.

11. Japanese taro potato (*sato-imo*)
Sticky potatoes, golfball-size with hairy peel. Stewed slightly sweet and salty with other vegetables in a slighty sweet and salty stock or used in *miso* soup.

12. Eggplant (*nasu, nasubi*)
About 1/4 the size of aubergine. Pickled in rice bran and salt in summer. Delicious fried or grilled. Also used in *miso* soup or stewed by itself or with chicken or fish.

13. Cucumber (*kyuri*)
Smaller, thinner than those in other countries. Seldom cooked but eaten raw in salads or pickled.

14. Japanese pumpkin (*kabocha*)
At the left in the photo is the traditional *kabocha*. It is soft and moist and less sweet than the other type. It is often cut into cubes with the skin on and cooked in a sweet sauce. On the right is a Western-style squash that is tasty in tempura and miso soup.

15. Japanese green peppers (*shishito*)
Small, finger-size green pepper with a soft texture. It is often grilled, or fried and cooked with its leaves.

16. Snow peas (*saya-endo*)
Best when freshly picked in spring. Used in egg dishes and miso soup, or as a garnish for its light green color.

17. Podded soybeans (*eda-mamé*)
Fresh soybeans in the pod, often sold still on branches. Pods are removed from branches, cooked in salt water. Popular snack to accompany beer in summer.

18. Dried shiitake mushrooms (*hoshi-shiitake*)
Sun-drying of shiitake not only preserves but increases flavor and vitamins. It is soaked in water before cooking, and the water is used as a stock.

19. Fresh shiitake mushrooms (*nama-shiitake*)
Grown or cultivated on tree trunks of shii tree. Never eaten raw but often grilled, fried, stewed or used in soup.

20. Shimeji mushrooms (*shimeji*)
Pleasant but light flavor. Often cooked with rice, boiled, or included in a cooked salad.

Vegetables & Nuts

Chrysanthemum leaves (*shungiku)*

Komatsuna (*komatsu-na)*

Leeks (*naga-negi)*

Spring onion (*wakegi)*

Japanese white radish (*daikon)*

Small turnips (*ko-kabu)*

Burdock (*gobo)*

Lotus root (*renkon, hasu)*

Bamboo shoots (*takenoko)*

Sweet potatoes (*satsuma-imo)*

Japanese taro potatoes (*sato-imo)*

Eggplants (*nasu, nasubi)*

Cucumbers (*kyuri)*

119

Japanese pumpkins (*kabocha*)

Japanese green peppers (*shishito*)

Snow peas (saya-endo)

Podded soybeans (*eda-mamé*)

Dried shiitake mushrooms (*hoshi-shiitake*)

Fresh shiitake mushrooms (*nama-shiitake*)

Shimeji mushrooms (*shimeji*)

Enoki mushrooms (*enoki-dake*)

Maitake mushrooms (*mai-take*)

Gingko nuts (*ginnan*)

Pickled Japanese plums (*umeboshi*)

Pickled ginger, sliced (*amazu-shoga*)

Salted cherry blossoms
(*sakura no shio-zuke*)

Adzuki red beans (*azuki*)

Dried gourd strips (*kampyo*)

21. Enoki mushrooms (*enoki-dake*)
Never eaten uncooked. Popular ingredient for *nabemono*, and often used in soup. Its unique texture adds appeal to dishes.

22. Maitake mushrooms (*mai-take*)
It's said that when farmers found this tasty mushroom, they danced for joy (*mai* means "dance"), thus giving this mushroom its name. It is usually cooked with rice or stir-fried.

23. Gingko nuts (*ginnan*)
The kernel of the plum-sized fruit of the gingko tree. Must remove shell with garlic crusher and peel thin skin to reach jade-green meat. Roasted and served with *yakitori*.

24. Pickled daikon radish (*takuan*)
Daikon radish is dried and placed in a fermenting mix of rice bran and salt. After about a month it is pickled and ready to eat. (No photo)

25. Pickled wild burdock (*yama-gobo*)
Wild burdock root is pickled in *miso*. Is sometimes used in rolled *sushi*. (No photo)

26. Pickled Japanese plums (*umeboshi*)
Japanese plums pickled only with salt and purple shiso, which colors the fruit and its brine deep red. It is typically used in rice balls (*onigiri*) and in dressings.

27. Pickled ginger (*amazu-shoga*)
Young ginger root is sliced and pickled in a sweet and sour blend of sugar, salt and vinegar. It is mainly served with *sushi*.

28. Salted cherry blossoms (*sakura no shio-zuke*)
Double cherry blossoms are heavily salted. The blossom is placed in a tea cup and boiling water is added. Served on auspicious occasions.

29. Adzuki beans (*azuki*)
Top of photo: can of boiled adzuki beans
Bottom right: canned boiled adzuki beans. Cooked with sugar. Often used in desserts.
Bottom left: dried adzuki beans. Must be soaked and cooked. Can be cooked with rice on happy occasions, or used to make sweet bean soup and sweet pastry fillings.

30. Dried gourd strips (*kampyo*)
The flesh of a gourd is scraped off in strips and dried. It is soaked in water and cooked with shoyu and sugar. Popular ingredient for rolled *sushi*.

V. Soybean Products and Vegetarian Ingredients

1. Flour gluten cake (*fu*)
Made from flour gluten and dried. Available in a variety of shapes and sizes. Soaked in water and added to *nabemono* and soups. Popular vegetarian food.

2. Tofu (*tofu*)
Top right of photo: thin fried tofu (*aburage*). Cooked in sweet sauce for sushi, stewed with vegetables or used in *miso* soup.
Top left: broiled hard tofu (*yaki-dofu*). Typically included in *nabemono* dishes like sukiyaki and shabu-shabu.
Middle: hard tofu (*momen-dofu*). Rough texture on top, resembles cotton cloth at sides. Eaten chilled as is or warmed and eaten with shoyu and condiments. Used in soup and *nabemono*.
Bottom left: soft tofu (*kinugoshi-dofu*). Smooth texture on all sides, softer than *momen-dofu*. Eaten chilled as is with shoyu and condiments, or cut into cubes and used in soup.

3. Freeze-dried tofu (*kori-dofu, koya-dofu*)
Regular tofu is frozen and dried. Soaked in hot water before cooking; spongy unless properly soaked. Cooked in sweet sauce for rolled *sushi*.

4. Soybean paste (*miso*)
Choose *miso* depending on your taste preferences and the other ingredients to be used.
Top left: chocolate color *miso* paste (*hatcho-miso, akadashi miso*)
Made using only soybeans and salt. Produced in Nagoya area. Often used in *miso* soup served after oily foods like tempura.
Top right: sweet *miso* paste from Kyoto (*Saikyo miso*)
Smooth and sweetened with liquid candy. Suitable for salad dressings.
Bottom right: light-colored *miso* paste (*shiro-miso*)
Miso made from more fermented rice than soybeans. Not necessarily less salty than darker *miso*. Used for soup and salad dressing.
Bottom left: dark-colored *miso* paste (*aka-miso*)
Miso made from more soybeans than fermented rice. Richer in flavor than light color *miso*.

5. Yam cake (*konnyaku*)
Made from yam potatoes. Very fibrous with rubbery texture. Has little flavor but is low in calories. Often stewed with meat and root vegetables.

Soybean Products & Vegetarian Ingredients

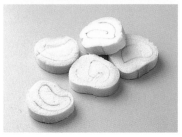

Flour gluten cakes (*fu*)

Freezed and dried tofu (*Koya-dofu*)

Yam cakes (*konnyaku*)

Top right: Thin-fried tofu (*aburage*)
Top left: Broiled hard tofu (*yaki-dofu*)
Middle: Hard tofu (*momen-dofu*)
Right: Soft tofu (*kinugoshi-dofu*)

Top left: Chocolate color *miso* paste (*hatcho miso*)
Top right: Kyoto *miso* paste (*Saikyo miso*)
Bottom left: Dark color *miso* paste (*aka-miso*)
Bottom right: Light color *miso* paste (*shiro-miso*)

VI. Flours & Noodles

1. Glutinous sweet rice flour (*shiratama-ko*)
Used in Japanese pastries and sweet dumplings. Mixed with cold water and rolled into small balls, boiled, chilled and served with sweetened adzuki beans.

2. Wheat flour noodles (*udon*)
Served in hot soup, or served cold with dipping sauce.
Right in photo: white dried noodles (*hoshi-udon*). Sold in bundles. To be cooked in boiling water.
Left: white noodles, boiled (*yude-udon*). Pre-cooked, ready to use. Sold in single-serving packs.

3. Dried buckwheat noodles (*hoshi-soba*)
Noodles made mainly from buckwheat flour. Color ranges from dark to light beige, depending on part of grain used.

4. Dried angel-hair noodles (*hoshi-somen*)
Generally served chilled in summer with dipping sauce. Best-tasting *somen* are kneaded and stretched by hand.

5. Bean threads (*harusamé*)
Made from green beans (*ryokuto*). Sold in dried form. Soaked in boiling water and popularly used in *nabemono* and salads.

6. Potato noodles (*kuzukiri*)
Originally made from arrowroot starch but now from potato starch. Are soaked in boiling water and often served chilled with a molasses-based sauce as a dessert. Also can be served in *nabemono*.

7. Yam noodles (*shirataki*)
Thread-like noodles made from yam cake (see page 121). Often eaten with sukiyaki, sukiyaki *domburi* and *niku-jaga*.

Flours & Noodles

Wheat flour noodles (*udon*)

Dried buckwheat noodles (*hoshi-soba*)

Dried angel-hair noodles (*hoshi-somen*)

Bean threads (*harusamé*)

Potato noodles (*kuzukiri*)

Yam noodles (*shirataki*)

Fruits

Japanese pears (*nashi*)

Tangerines (*mikan*)

Persimmons (*kaki*)

Kogyoku apples (*kogyoku ringo*)

Summer orange (*natsu-mikan*)

VII. Fruits

1. Japanese pears (*nashi*)
Available from summer through mid-autumn. Looks like an apple but tastes more like a pear. Sweet, crisp and juicy, it is never cooked.

2. Tangerines (*mikan*)
Most popular fruit all winter long. Thin skin is easy to peel. Sweet and juicy inside.

3. Persimmons (*kaki*)
Favorite autumn fruit, it is sweet and crunchy. Bitter persimmons are sweetened and softened with small amounts of white liquor and stored in airtight containers.

4. Kogyoku apples (*kogyoku*)
Sweet and sour like a Jonathan apple. Best Japanese apple for cooking.

5. Summer orange (*natsu-mikan*)
Available from late-spring through mid-summer. Used to make juice and rind for marmalade. It contains vitamin B and P.

Sukiyaki

Continued from page 51.
4 Have each guest break an egg into his or her serving bowl and stir it gently with chopsticks. Each guest should pick up meat or vegetables from the pot with chopsticks, dip them in the egg and eat them.
5 While cooking, the host or hostess should push the cooked ingredients to one side of the pot and continually add more ingredients to the pot. If the cooking stock becomes reduced while simmering, add water, but be sure to also add shoyu, sugar and saké accordingly, so that the stock does not become overly diluted.

Note: Keep any leftover cooked ingredients and reheat them with additional water and seasonings; they will taste delicious. My husband especially likes to cook leftover rice or cooked noodles with the remaining sukiyaki stock.

Rolled *Sushi*

Continued from page 81.
Lift up the end of the mat closest to you and roll the *nori* laver and ingredients towards the far end, holding the stuffing ingredients firmly in place with your hands as you roll. When you have almost finished rolling, lift up the end of the mat with your right hand while rolling with your left to make sure the mat is not rolled inside the *sushi* roll. Press down firmly to affix the *nori* laver ends to the roll.   (Pictures 3–4)
10 Slice the rolls into pieces 2 cm (¾ inches) thick and serve with pickled ginger slices.

It is nearly impossible to roll *sushi* perfectly the first time you try it. If you got it right the first time, you are either lucky or very talented. If not, just keep practicing; a symmetrical, firmly packed sushi roll will come with time.

Cold Buckwheat Noodles and Tempura

Continued from page 82.
1 cup cake flour, sifted
8 prawns, shelled and deveined, with
   tails retained
8 green *shiso* leaves

1 In a frying pan, heat oil to 170°C/365°F.
2 Beat the egg in a measuring cup, add cold water to reach 1 cup in volume and mix thoroughly. Transfer to a mixing bowl. Add flour and mix roughly with the thick end of cooking chopsticks. Mix only until the batter is half mixed and not yet smooth. It may still contain lumps and some unmixed flour.
3 Holding them by their tails, dip the prawns individually in the batter to coat thoroughly and slide them into the oil. Fry for 2 minutes and then remove, draining the oil.

Soba Noodles:
400 g/14 oz dried buckwheat noodles (*soba*)
Boiling water for cooking noodles

1 Fill a large pan with water and heat. Add the dried noodles after separating them by hand, and stir until the water is nearly a boil. Turn down the heat so the pot does not boil over and cook a few more minutes. Taste one strand of noodles to check for doneness; the texture should be firm (al dente).
2 Fill a large mixing bowl with cold water while the noodles are cooking. Drain the noodles in a colander. Dip the colander with the noodles in the cold water and drain quickly. Rinse the noodles in running cold water to remove the starch. Drain well, shaking the colander a few times, and place the noodles in individual serving dishes.
3 Place the condiments and tempura in separate dishes. Pour ½ cup of the dipping sauce in individual bowls and serve along with the noodles.

Japanese Traditional Cooking Utensils

1. Cutting knives and wooden cutting board
Left in photo: knife for preparing fish (*deba-bocho*)
Middle: three-way knife for fish, meat and vegetables (*santoku-bocho*)
Right: knife for slicing fish fillets for *sashimi* (*yanagi-bocho*)

2. Single-handled cooking pan (*yukihira-nabe*) and drop lid (*otoshi-buta*)

3. Earthenware pot for tabletop cooking (*donabe*)

4. Shabu-shabu pot (*hokozu*)

5. Omelet pan (*tamago-yaki-ki*)

6. Grilling utensils

Top in photo: skewer holder (*tetsukyu*) and skewers (*kanagushi*)
Bottom: heat expander and rack (*yaki-ami*)

7. Wooden rice container (*ohitsu*), see page 76

8. Sushi-rice utensils
Top in photo: flat paper fan (*uchiwa*)
Bottom: wooden mixing bowl (*handai*) and spatula (*shamoji*)

9. Grinding bowl—mortar—(*suribachi*) and pestle (*surikogi*)

10. Rolling mat (*maki-su*) and cooking towel (*fukin*)

Cutting knives and wooden board

Single-handled cooking pan and drop lid

Earthenware pot (*donabe*)

Shabu-shabu pot (*hokozu*)

Omelet pan

Skewer holder and heat expander

Uchiwa, wooden mixing bowl and spatula

Grinding bowl and pestle

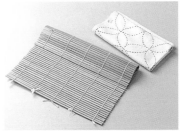

Rolling mat and cooking towel

COMMON COOKING PROCEDURES

Cleaning and Filleting a Whole Fish

There are several different ways to fillet a whole fish, depending on the shape of the fish. A flat fish like a flounder is usually filleted in four portions. Relatively soft fish like sardine may be filleted with the fingers only, without using a knife. Here I will explain how to clean and fillet a horse mackerel, a popular fish in Japanese cuisine. This method can be applied to the majority of types of fish.

Horse mackerel differ from other fish in that they have few scales where most fish have them, but the horse mackerel features a unique row of scales traversing its body, from head to tail.

1 Remove the hard scales lying in a row by inserting a knife between the scales and the flesh from the tail end going towards the head. Turn the fish over and do the same on the other side. Scrape the surface of the entire body gently with the back of a knife to scale. (Picture 1)

2 Insert the knife beneath the pectoral fin and slice halfway down. Turn the fish over and repeat on the other side to remove the head. (Picture 2)

3 Score the skin on the stomach side down to the ventral fin to open up the fish and scrape out the gut with the tip of a knife. Rinse the fish with cold water to wash clean and dry with paper towels. (Picture 3)

4 Insert the knife between the upper flesh and the backbone, and slide the knife down to the tail to cut away one fillet. (Pictures 4–5)

5 Place the fish skin side up with the backbone down. Insert the knife between the flesh and the bone and slide the knife along the bone down to the tail to cut away another fillet. Now you have two fillets and the backbone. (Picture 6)

6 To remove small bones on the stomach side, slice them off using the tip of a knife. Do the same to the other fillet. (Picture 7)

Cleaning and Preparing Shrimp

If the shrimp still has its head on, you can easily devein it by pulling the head away from the body. If the head has already been removed, stick a toothpick between any two sections of the shell at the midpoint of the shrimp and lift it up gently. The vein will come off on the toothpick.

(Picture 1)

Then scrape the tail with the tip of a knife to remove any lingering dirt and cut off the top of the tail to improve the appearance of the shrimp.

(Picture 2)

Gutting and Skinning Squid

The skin of the squid is too tough to chew, so it is removed, especially when it is eaten raw as *sashimi* or *sushi*. Since the skin turns purple when it is cooked, it is desirable for appearance's sake to skin squid before cooking it. Remember that the tentacles and the gut are connected in the trunk. By pulling off the tentacles, therefore, we can simultaneously gut the squid.

1 Insert your index finger between the trunk and the tentacles to loosen the connective tissue.

(Picture 1).

2 Pull the tentacles off the trunk so that the gut is also pulled out. Remove the remaining viscera with your fingers and rinse out the trunk with cold water. (Picture 2–3)

3 Remove the triangular section of the squid before skinning the trunk. Insert your fingers between this triangular section and the trunk.

(Picture 4)

4 Pull the triangular section off. In the process, some of the skin will peel off from the trunk.

(Picture 5)

5 Pinch the skin where it has loosened with a paper towel and slowly pull it off. (Picture 6)

Washing Rice

1 Place the rice in a large mixing bowl. Use a large bowl even if you will only prepare 2 cups of rice. Pour in a large amount of water (Picture 1) and mix the rice quickly (Picture 2). Drain off the water. Most dust, bran and other foreign matter which may have been mixed with the rice will be washed away with the milky white water at this stage.

2 After draining off the water, rub the rice kernels together lightly with your hands, repeating your actions several times until all of the grains have been rubbed together (Picture 3). If you find that the water remaining at the bottom of the bowl is quite milky, pour in cold water and mix lightly. Drain off the water again.

3 Change the water several times, rubbing the grains lightly together each time until the water runs clear (Picture 4).

4 Drain the rice in a colander (Picture 5) and soak it in the amount of cold water needed for cooking for at least 30 minutes before starting to cook.

The key to washing rice is to do these procedures quickly, or the rice will absorb the smell of the bran and too much water while it is being washed. Try to remove any other foreign matter that may be present, such as bits of rock, while you wash the rice.

Preparing Plain Rice (*Gohan*)

Most Japanese cook rice in an electric rice cooker. When one is not available, cook rice in the following way.

4 servings
2½ cups Japanese rice (*komé*), washed and
  drained
2½ cups cold water for boiling

Place the rice in a thick, heavy pan, measure in an amount of water equal to that of the rice and let stand for at least 30 minutes. Cover and cook over medium low heat. Just before boiling, raise the heat. When boiling, reduce the heat to very low. Simmer for 20 minutes until all the liquid is absorbed. Raise the heat again and cook for 10 seconds. Turn off the heat. Insert a paper towel between the pan and the lid to absorb the moisture from the steam and to prevent water on the lid from dripping onto the rice. Let stand for 20 minutes before serving.

JAPANESE STOCKS (*Dashi*)

DRIED FISH FLAKES (*Kezuri-bushi*)

The *dashi* prepared with dried fish flakes is simple to make and can be prepared almost instantly. When you buy fish flakes, however, you have to be careful. *Kezuri-bushi* means "flakes of dried fish fillets," and the flakes are made from the dried fillets of different fish. The best quality flakes are made from dried bonito, *kezuri-gatsuo*. I will therefore discuss *kezuri-gatsuo* first.

Dried Bonito Flakes
(*Kezuri-gatsuo, hana-gatsuo*)
Dashi made with this material is used widely. Since it is easy to prepare and has a refined taste, it can be used with almost any ingredients. It does not greatly change the original taste or flavor of the ingredients you are cooking but instead helps to extract the flavor, while adding an extra tang of its own.

To produce bonito flakes, a fresh whole bonito is headed, gutted and tailed. It is cut lengthwise into four fillets and then boiled once. The boiled bonito fillets are sun-dried and smoked several times until mold no longer appears on their surface. As this drying and smoking process is repeated for a period of about a year, the bonito fillets gradually get firmer and darker in color, and eventually they come to resemble a slab of oak wood. The best bonito comes from the province of Tosa on the Pacific coast of Shikoku island.

It is best if you can shave this smoked and dried bonito fillet into flakes right before it is used to make *dashi*. However, you need a special shaving utensil and, of course, it takes a little time and labor to produce the flakes. As already shaved dried bonito is now available on the market, it is used widely.

Dried bonito flakes are usually sold in a plastic bag filled with nitrogen gas in the dried food section of grocery stores together with other soup stock materials. The good fresh bonito flakes are deep red in color. If they look beige or pale, they may already be old and have probably lost their flavor.

Finely shaved bonito flakes are also available, packed in small (5 x 1 0 cm/2 x 4 inches) plastic bags for individual use at the table. They are sprinkled on top of various foods like uncooked, chilled tofu and spinach salad before eating, and are not suitable for making *dashi*.

Preparing bonito stock—*katsuo dashi* (4 cups):
$4\frac{1}{3}$ cups boiling water
2 cups dried bonito flakes (*kezuri-gatsuo*), unpacked

To boiling water in a soup pan add bonito flakes and boil for 10 seconds. Turn off the heat and let stand for 1 minute. Strain the stock through a strainer lined with a cheesecloth.

Thick Bonito Flakes (*Atsu-kezuri*):
There is a type of dried bonito flakes which are shaved much thicker than regular dried bonito flakes. These flakes are used for making *dashi* for noodles in soup and for dipping sauce for noodles. They have a stronger flavor than thin flakes and look much darker and redder in color.

Preparing thick bonito flake *dashi* (4 cups):
5 cups boiling water
l cup thick bonito flakes (*atsu-kezuri*)

Boil water in a soup pan. Add thick bonito flakes and keep boiling over medium heat for 7 minutes. Strain the stock through a strainer lined with a cheesecloth.

Mixed Dried Fish Flakes
(*Kongo Kezuri-bushi*)
Mixed dried fish flakes are a mixture of flakes of several different blue-skinned fish such as horse mackerel, mackerel, sardine and bonito. It thus has a more complicated and stronger flavor than flakes made from one species of fish such as bonito. It also has more of a fishy smell than bonito flakes, but that can be eliminated by adding a small amount of saké to the *dashi* after it is strained.

The *dashi* from the mixed fish flakes is often used for *miso* soup with root vegetables such as *daikon* radish, turnip and burdock root, and to boil these vegetables. It is also suitable for noodles in soup.

The flakes look lighter in color than bonito flakes—almost yellow—and are smaller in size. They are typically packed in plastic bags and displayed on the same shelf as bonito flakes, so take care to ensure that you make the correct purchase.

The mixed flakes should be slightly less expensive than the others.

Preparing stock from dried mixed fish flakes (4 cups):

4¼ cups boiling water
1½ cups mixed fish flakes (*kongo kezuri-bushi*)
2 tablespoons saké

To boiling water in a soup pan, add the flakes and boil for I minute. Turn off the heat and strain the stock through a strainer lined with a cheesecloth. Pour the stock back into the pan, add saké and bring to a boil again.

Useful information:
• After straining, avoid squeezing the used flakes in the cheesecloth for added flavor, as this would add a harsh flavor that would spoil the taste of the stock.
• Do not compress or pack down the flakes when you measure them in a measuring cup, or you may end up adding too many of these light, airy flakes.
• Less expensive dried fish flakes are most likely to be either mixed flakes or from fish other than bonito.

DRIED KELP (*Dashi-kombu*)

The Japanese word for dried kelp is *kombu* or *kobu*. *Kombu* is a sea vegetable which grows in the ocean, but the best *kombu* for making *dashi* is harvested from cold northern waters. *Kombu* commonly grows about 10 m/30 feet in length and about 30 cm/12 inches in width. After it is removed from the ocean, it is dried in the sun.

Good kelp for making *dashi* are "branded" with the names of the locations where they are harvested. The wide, thick *kombu* known as Rishiri *kombu*, for example, is harvested in the ocean near the island called Rishiri in Hokkaido and is dried there. Among other names which are found in the market, I would recommend Rausu, the widest and thickest *kombu*, and Hidaka, the most popular and economical kelp variety for home cooking. These are all from Hokkaido.

A variety of packaged kelp is displayed on the shelves in the dried food (*kanbutsu*) section of the market. You may wonder which to buy. Generally, wider, thicker kelp has richer and better flavor than narrow, thin kelp. You may have to use more narrow thin kelp than the thick wide *kombu* to make the same quantity of *dashi* of similar flavor.

Unlike the sardine and bonito, the kelp is a vegetable, so it (along with *shiitake* mushrooms) has been widely used in the culinary practices of Buddhist priests, who are usually vegetarians.

Actually, however, we also use the *dashi* made only from kelp for a variety of dishes. Kelp extract has a mild flavor which is suitable to cook something which has a good, distinctive taste such as shellfish. For *miso* soup with sea clams, the kelp stock is ideal. In one-pot cooking (*nabemono*) at the table, for such dishes as shabu-shabu, we prepare a weak kelp-based stock.

Preparing kelp stock (*kombu dashi*):

There are two ways to prepare this *kombu dashi*, by soaking or by cooking. When you have time, try the soaking method. When soaking kelp in water, its flavor is extracted gradually, which makes for better tasting stock.

Soaking Method (4 cups):
2 (10 cm/4 inch square) pieces of dried kelp
  (*dashi-kombu*)
4⅛ cups cold water

Soak kelp in cold water overnight or for 5 to 6 hours. Remove the kelp. Use the soaking water as the stock.

Cooking Method (4 cups):
2 (10 cm/4 inch square) pieces of dried kelp,
  (*dashi-kombu*)
4½ cups cold water

Place cold water and kelp in a soup pan and let them stand for 15 minutes. Cook over low-medium heat. Remove the kelp right before boiling.

NUMBER ONE *DASHI* STOCK (*Ichiban Dashi*)

Of all the Japanese stocks, the best is *ichiban dashi*, a stock made from a combination of bonito flakes and kelp. When the recipes in this book refer to "*dashi*," I always mean *ichiban-dashi*, Number One stock.

Dried bonito flake stock and kelp stock are both flavorful stocks when made separately. They have discrete tastes because they are different extracts. When they are mixed, however, they produce another unique and probably more delicious flavor. This mixed *dashi* is good for almost all Japanese dishes. That is why the stock from both kelp and bonito flakes is named Number One Stock (*Ichiban Dashi*).

Preparing Number One *Dashi* Stock (4 cups):
4¼ cups cold water
1 (10 cm/4 inch square) piece dried kelp
  (*dashi-kombu*)
2 cups thin dried bonito flakes (*kezuri-gatsuo*),
  unpacked

1 In a soup pan, place cold water and dried kelp and allow to be soaked for 15 minutes.
2 Cook over medium-low heat. Remove the kelp right before boiling and add the bonito flakes. Bring to a boil and keep at a rolling boil for 10 seconds.
3 Let stand for 2 minutes and strain through a strainer lined with a cheesecloth. Discard the bonito flakes remaining in the cheesecloth; do not squeeze them.

Shortcut:
MSG (monosodium glutamate) is a crystallized version of the flavor essence of kelp, although some people do not like it. If you wish, you can add MSG to the soup stock prepared with dried-bonito flakes to obtain a flavor fairly close to the taste of Number One stock.

Storage:
Any homemade stock tastes best when it is freshly made. However, should you have any leftover stock, you can refrigerate it for later use. It keeps well for a week in a refrigerator, or even longer if you reboil it. You could also freeze it in an ice tray.

STOCK FROM BOILED AND DRIED SARDINES

Most Westerners have never tasted stock made from this ingredient. Until the past few decades, when sardines were harvested in abundance near Japan, *niboshi*, or boiled and dried sardines, had been the most popular source of homemade stock for Japanese.

To make *niboshi*, young, tiny whole sardines about 5 cm/2 inch in length are boiled and completely dried in the sun. *Niboshi* should be firm to the touch and in perfect shape.

When fresh, they have gleaming silver-toned stomachs and dark blue backs. They are usually packed in 200 g/8 oz plastic bags and are sold in the dried food section of grocery stores together with other stock materials, such as dried kelp and dried bonito flakes.

The stock made from *niboshi* has a distinctive fish smell, especially when whole sardines are used. If you remove the heads and guts before you use the *niboshi*, however, you will produce a better-tasting stock. A small amount of saké is also helpful in eliminating much of the fishy odor.

This stock is used for *miso* (soybean paste) soup with root vegetables, for stewing vegetables and other dishes.

Preparing Sardine-based Stock (4 cups):
4½ cups cold water
1 cup of boiled and dried sardines (*niboshi*),
  headed and gutted
1 tablespoon saké

1 Place cold water and sardines in a soup pan and let stand for 10 minutes. Cook, uncovered, over medium heat until the water comes to a boil. Reduce the heat to low so that the sardines slowly revolve in the water. Continue to cook for 10 minutes or until the sardines are soft when pinched with fingers.
2 Strain the stock through a strainer lined with a cheesecloth and add sake.

Microwave Oven Method
Place water and sardines in a microwave-safe glass mixing bowl and micro-cook, uncovered, on a high setting for 10 minutes. Strain through a strainer lined with a cheesecloth and add saké.

PREPARING 3½ CUPS OF JAPANESE *DASHI* STOCK
(*Dashi*)

You will probably find that 3½ cups of stock is the optimal amount for preparing soup for 4 persons. This recipe calls for 4 cups of water to produce 3½ cups of stock. This is because both stock ingredients are dried seafood. They absorb some of the liquid, and some evaporates during cooking.

Take care not to compress or pack the bonito flakes when you place them in a measuring cup.

1 piece (10 cm /4 inch square) dried kelp for
  stock (*dashi-kombu*), see page 112
4 cups cold water
2 cups dried bonito flakes (*kezuri-gatsuo* or
  hanagatsuo), see page 112

1 Soak the dried kelp in cold water for at least 15 minutes, or until it doubles in size.   (Picture 2)
2 Cook the kelp and water over medium-low

heat and remove the kelp right before boiling to prevent it from flavoring the stock too strongly.

(Picture 3)

3 Add the bonito flakes to the stock and boil for 10 seconds. Turn off the heat and set aside for 1 minute. (Picture 4)

4 Strain the stock through a strainer lined with a cheesecloth. This strained liquid is Number One stock (*ichiban dashi*). (Picture 5)

Avoid squeezing the bonito flakes in the cheesecloth to produce more stock, as this will add a harsh flavor that will spoil the stock.

SEASONING AGENTS (*Chomiryo*)

In addition to salt, sugar and vinegar, which are widely used in cuisines throughout the world, there are several other seasonings which are only found in Japanese cooking. These include Japanese soy sauce (*shoyu*), soybean paste (*miso*), sweet rice wine for cooking (*mirin*) and Japanese rice wine (*saké*). I will introduce them and their use in this chapter.

From my cooking classes for foreign residents, I found that even the salt, sugar and vinegar commonly used in Japan have a slightly different taste than the seasonings found in other countries. I will therefore try to describe these seasonings briefly in this chapter as well.

Also in this chapter is an introduction to the oils and flours commonly used in Japan. Actually, these are used much more widely than just as seasoning agents, but because they are used to lend

certain flavors, tastes and texture to different foods, I thought they should be included here.

Additional knowledge about all of these elements will help you to understand, appreciate and reproduce the subtle tastes and flavors that characterize Japanese cuisine. In summary, the seasonings which will be introduced are as follows:

Rice wine (*saké*)
Salt (*shio*)
Soybean paste (*miso*)
Soy sauce (*shoyu*)
Sugar (*sato*)
Sweet rice wine (*mirin*)
Vinegar (*su*)
Fats and oils (*abura*)
Flours and Starches (*kona* or *ko*)

RICE WINE (*Saké*)

Japanese cuisine, as in the West, uses wine in the cooking process. However, instead of grape wine, Japanese cooking uses domestic rice wine, or saké.

Regular Rice Wine (*saké* or *seishu*)

The most common alcoholic beverage in Japan, saké is also an important ingredient in Japanese cuisine. Japan produces an amazing variety of rice wines, but some are better than others for use in cooking.

Until 1992, when a 3% consumption tax was implemented, Japanese saké was graded by the government, with the finest wines given the 1st class ranking—and priced accordingly. At that time, I often used 2nd class saké for my daily cooking, as I knew that some brewers did not apply for 1st class ranking for tax reasons, so some 2nd class saké was as good as the 1st class wine, but less expensive. Today, instead of ranks, consumers distinguish saké varieties according to price. Brewers of high-priced saké purport to have employed genuine, traditional methods to brew their wine, using only the best, innermost part of top quality rice grains. But for cooking wine, more modest, inexpensive brands are actually superior, as expensive saké typically uses too much polished rice, causing the wine to lose much of the distinctive saké flavor necessary for cooking.

Among the different brands you can find some slightly sweet saké (*amakuchi*) and some slightly dry (*karakuchi*), although the range between the two is not as great as with grape wines. Dry saké, generally, is better for cooking. Saké is sold at liquor stores and supermarkets licensed to sell alcoholic beverages. You cannot find it at ordinary grocery stores.

We use rice wine in cooking for more than its distinctive flavor alone. When added during cooking, saké can actually eliminate the fishy or poultry smell of certain dishes, which many people find unpleasant. We thus use it mainly in cooking fish, meat and poultry. You will find that the addition of saké often distinctly improves the taste of these dishes.

From my own experience, I would recommend that anyone purchasing saké for Japanese cooking buy at a liquor store the smallest available bottle of reasonably priced, dry (*karakuchi*) rice wine for drinking rather than the "cooking saké" sold at supermarkets. Take note of the wine's brand name if you like it; if not, experiment with other brands until you find one you enjoy.

Cooking Rice Wine (*ryori-yo saké*)

Besides the regular *saké* sold at liquor stores, you can also find what is called "cooking saké" (*ryori-yo saké*) at grocery stores and supermarkets. Although it is called saké, it contains very little alcohol. Since it is not classified as an alcoholic beverage, this "rice wine" can be sold by vendors who lack a liquor license.

In fact, alcohol is not always necessary for Japanese cooking. Before it is used in cooking, saké is often boiled to evaporate the alcohol it contains. Rice wine's most important contribution to Japanese cooking is its distinctive flavor, not its alcohol content. However, cooking saké typically contains additives not found in ordinary rice wine, including a stock made from kelp and often even salt. Because cooking saké is less expensive than ordinary rice wine, many consumers buy it, but if you use it in cooking Japanese dishes, remember to reduce the amount of salt in your recipe.

SALT (*Shio*)

Salt is salt, I thought — what can I say that's new about the salt available in Japan? Actually, though, there are several types of salt used in Japanese cuisine, and they deserve some explanation. Historically in Japan, salt was collected from sea water by drying it on the beach at special salt farms along the Inland Sea coast. This method of making salt was discontinued in 1971 and the coastal areas redeveloped for housing and industrial use. But the Japanese government recognized the vital role salt plays in maintaining life and in many industrial areas, and it designated salt as a product to be manufactured and sold—along with tobacco—only by a government-run monopoly. The Japan Salt and Tobacco Corporation was privatized in 1985, but it continues to monopolize domestic salt production. Salt production in Japan was completely privatized in 1997.

At any rate, today salt in Japan is made from crude salt imported from China and India and more recently from Mexico and Australia. The imported crude salt is refined to make various types of salt to meet different needs. At Japanese groceries, you can purchase table salt in small glass jars, cooking salt in plastic bags or boxes, and pickling salt in plastic bags.

Table Salt (*shokutaku-en*)

You do not usually find a jar or salt shaker of table salt on the dining table in Japanese homes, but

133

you will often see one on the table at a restaurant. Salt in a small jar is also convenient for sprinkling over the food being cooked to adjust its taste. Yet keep in mind that the salt in this jar contains additives to keep it dry and free-flowing, so that it can be sprinkled easily and smoothly. These additives can cause soup or other liquids to become cloudy, so I don't recommend that you use this salt for cooking clear soups.

Cooking Salt (*shoku-en*)
You can also purchase highly purified (99.0%—99.5% pure), snow-white salt for cooking, available in plastic bags of varying sizes (300g/1^1/4 lb, 500g/2 lb, 1 kg/4 lb). This salt is also dry and free flowing, but it contains minimal additives, so it does not cause clouding of clear soups.

Pickling Salt (*ara-jio*)
To satisfy the nostalgic longing for the taste of salt produced by traditional methods, you can also purchase salt of lower purity (95% pure) and sold as a "natural salt." This salt is typically used for preserving various types of seafood and vegetables and in the manufacture of soy sauce. At home, it is used to pickle vegetables, with the expectation that the 5% impurities will give the vegetables a bit of extra flavor. This salt is made by adding brine (the residue from crystallizing salt from sea water) to purified salt, or by the traditional method which produces salt containing various minerals. The latter is still made on some small southern Japanese islands.

Seasoned Salt (*aji-shio*)
You will often find at the Japanese table a salt product in a glass jar that contains flavoring and seasoning agents, like MSG. Because Japanese rarely keep salt on the table at home but often keep a jar of MSG or similar flavoring agents close at hand, for sprinkling over pickled vegetables and other dishes, I assume that the company marketing this product hoped to increase the use of table salt by adding flavoring agents to it.

Mixed Salt and Sesame Seeds (*Goma-jio*)
A popular salt product that can be found in small glass jars or plastic bags, *goma-jio* is salt containing roasted black sesame seeds. It is commonly sprinkled over steamed glutinous rice (*okowa*).

Other Salts
In addition to the above, you can also buy a type of salt that is enriched with calcium. Garlic salt and onion salt are also available, but still rather uncommon. Some foreign residents in Japan hunt for iodized salt, but it is not produced in Japan. The reason? Most Japanese eat plenty of sea vegetables, which are high in iodine; they have no need for additional iodine.

SOYBEAN PASTE (*Miso*)

A look at the surprising variety of soybean paste (*miso*) on the shelves in a Japanese grocery or supermarket might leave you puzzled as which one to buy to make such dishes as *miso* soup. Just as Europeans treasure their homemade cheeses, many Japanese families have traditionally made their own soybean paste, which they insist tastes the best, as the phrase *temae miso* ("my own *miso*") implies.

Even today, you will find rural groceries that sell *miso* made according to recipes handed down for generations. Some of them have become successful enough to market their products widely and you can now see these local specialties in large urban department stores and supermarkets as well.

From a practical cooking standpoint, all the *miso* on the market can be classified into roughly four different types, according to color:
Light brown (beige) — *shiro miso*
Dark brown (brown) — *aka miso*
Sweet beige — *saikyo miso*
Chocolate color—*hatcho miso* or *akadashi miso*

I usually explain *miso* to foreign students by noting that the *mi* of *miso* means "three" and the *so* means "elements." *Miso* is generally made with three major ingredients: soy beans, rice malt and salt. As the ratio of soybeans to the other ingredients in the mixture increases, the color becomes darker, and vice versa. In Southwestern Japan, barley is sometimes used instead of rice in *miso*. This *miso* is called *mugi miso* (barley *miso*).

Dark versus Light *Miso*
You may think that *miso* that is dark in color is saltier in taste than lighter-colored *miso*. Actually, though, the color of *miso* has little to do with its salty taste; in fact, some light brown *miso* is saltier than dark brown *miso*. To ensure that the *miso* will preserve well, its salt content is typically at least 13–14%, but because of recent concern about the high salt intake, you can also purchase low-salt *miso* (*teien miso*) containing about 10% salt. *Miso*

with still lower salt content is also available. This *genen miso* (reduced-salt *miso*) contains 6.3% or lower levels of salt.

In general, dark color *miso* (*aka miso*) has a more distinctive flavor than lighter varieties (*shiro miso*). My suggestion therefore is that you should use a darker-colored *miso* if you want to weaken or counter the smell of the food you are cooking, such as fish or poultry. If you want to retain the original flavor and color of the food you are cooking, however, you should use a lighter-colored *miso*.

Miso is a natural fermentation product containing yeast or malt. Most *miso* sold today contains labeling on the package claiming that no food additives are used (*mutenka*). This *miso* thus must be refrigerated to retard fermentation.

Since it ferments, *miso* gets darker in color as it ages. To counter this color change, which is caused by the yeast, producers often add a small amount of alcohol—which controls yeast activity—to the *miso*. *Miso* that does not contain yeast gradually darkens in color as it ages, but its taste become mellow and rounded.

Hatcho Miso or Akadashi Miso

The darkest, chocolate-color *miso*, a Nagoya variety usually called *hatcho miso* or *akadashi miso*, is actually made only from soybean and salt. The whitest one is the *miso* from the Kyoto area called *saikyo miso*, which uses about twice as much rice as soybeans.

Nagoya's chocolate-color *miso*, called *hatcho miso* or *akadashi miso*, is often used to make a *miso* soup called *akadashi*. This soup is commonly served at the end of a meal of tempura, or deep-fried breaded seafood and vegetables, because it is said that it cleanses an oily palate. This *miso* is also often used to make Japanese salad dressings and dipping sauces for vegetable dishes.

Saikyo Miso

Sweet white *miso* from Kyoto, or *saikyo miso*, is usually used to make Kyoto-style *miso* soups. This soup is served at most restaurants in Kyoto, at restaurants serving Kyoto-style dishes, and at home by people from the Kyoto area. At my home, where we enjoy the traditional tastes of Kyoto, I make the first meal of the year on New Year's Day, an *ozoni* soup with rice cake and vegetables, using this *miso*. *Saikyo miso* is made by adding to a light-brown *miso* some syrup (*mizu-amé* or liquid candy) to make it sweet. As a result, it becomes slightly sticky. It also includes some preservatives and a bleaching agent to preserve its white color. By combining this *miso* with ground sesame seeds, you can make a delicious dressing that goes well with both fresh and boiled vegetables.

Preparing Soup with Miso

It may be like crying over spilt milk, but you can do little but cry over soup in which you have put too much *miso*. If you add water, you simply dilute the *dashi* stock and the soup will come to taste too thin. I always tell my cooking students that they should first add slightly less *miso* than called for in the recipe. Check the taste, and add little by little until you are satisfied with the taste. Be sure to stir well as you add *miso* to the soup.

To make a really flavorful, delicious *miso* soup, we blend more than one type of *miso*. I usually blend a light with a dark *miso*, using equal quantities of each.

New Types of Miso

While some people advocate anything natural and without additives or preservatives, others value convenience above all, and they will try anything that saves them time and labor.

People show this same difference of opinion in regard to *miso*. A new convenience product is now on the market, *dashi-iri miso*, or *miso* containing Japanese stock, or *dashi*. With this *miso* product you need not make the stock for your *miso* soup. It comes in a soft plastic bottle. The directions on the label read, "Squeeze out 9 cm/3½ inch of the *miso* into a soup bowl and dilute with plain hot water to produce soup for one person." This did not sound terribly tempting, but I tried it once just out of curiosity. I found that it may be satisfactory for a picnic or when camping, but I wouldn't serve it to my guests, students or family.

SOY SAUCE (*Shoyu*)

Soy sauce, or *shoyu*, is probably the best-known and most commonly used seasoning agent for giving food a distinctively Japanese flavor. Shoyu is a brewed liquid made primarily from soy beans, wheat and salt. It adds to food a salty taste, good flavor and pleasant aroma, and it counters the unpleasant smells of such foods as meat and fish. It is the combination of various amino acids that makes soy sauce so tasty.

There are three main types of soy sauce on the market in Japan today:

Regular soy sauce (*Koikuchi shoyu*):

This type is most widely used for cooking and table use. It contains about 15% salt. There are innumerable brands of regular soy sauce, in part because every town and village in Japan used to have at least one native *shoyu* brewer. Those who can distinguish tastes clearly usually prefer a favorite brand. When I got married, we lived right in front of a *shoyu* brewer, and we liked his brand the best of all those in town. Since moving to the Tokyo area, I have been using a type of shoyu brewed on a small island in the Inland Sea called Shodo-shima. Even in Tokyo, we can purchase local, specialty *shoyu*, but we have greater access to them in outlying towns and cities.

Lightly salted soy sauce (*Gen-en shoyu*):

The salt content of this type of *shoyu* is half of that of regular soy sauce, or 7.5%. This sauce is made by desalting regular soy sauce. This is why *gen-en shoyu* is slightly more expensive.

Light-colored soy sauce (*Usukuchi shoyu*)

Light-colored is different from lightly salted soy sauce, although the two are often confused and some people assume that light-colored *shoyu* contains less salt than regular soy sauce. In fact, light-colored soy sauce contains a little more salt than regular *shoyu*—16.5%. To avoid too salty a taste, we should use slightly less of it than we would regular soy sauce.

The food cooked with light-colored soy sauce is much less affected by the color of the soy sauce and it retains much of its original color. Food cooked with regular soy sauce, though, becomes darker in color because of the soy sauce, so it may look less attractive. Light-colored soy sauce is used in the kitchen for cooking clear soup and for preparing stewed meat, chicken and vegetables, and similar dishes, but it is not found at the table. This is a cooking soy sauce and is not intended for table consumption, e.g. as a dipping sauce for slices of raw fish (*sashimi*).

Light-colored soy sauce (*Usukuchi shoyu*) is commonly found in the Osaka-Kyoto area of Western Japan, where cooks aim to retain the original colors of cooked food and table condiments. This preference is deeply felt, as my husband and I realized when we received a bottle of home-made shoyu from a Kyoto-born artist friend one day. When we looked at the bottle, we saw that he had produced light-colored soy sauce at home. Our friend, who now lives in the country and eats mainly natural foods, had a deep longing for light *shoyu*, but it was difficult for him to procure it so far away from home, so he made his own.

You can find other kinds of soy sauce that are infrequently used but are appropriate for special occasions. For example, *tamari joyu* is a thick soy sauce often used for dipping *sashimi*. You can not easily find it at a grocery store; my favorite brand, which is from my uncle's *shoyu* brewery in Kyoto, is sometimes sold at Kyoto Fairs at department stores in Tokyo. Another unusual variety is a soy sauce brewed with oysters, a special *shoyu* with a unique flavor that is brewed by a family in Shikoku. I use this *shoyu* when we have guests at home. There are many other types made by local brewers which have gained the proud allegiance of nearby residents. As I travel to various cities and towns throughout Japan, I often stop at local stores and try to find unique local soy sauces.

Outside Japan, soy sauce prepared by Chinese is often sold together with Japanese soy sauce. Chinese soy sauce is generally thicker and has a different taste from the *shoyu* produced in Japan.

SUGAR (*Sato*)

The role of sugar in Japanese cooking is slightly different from its role in cooking in the West. In Western dining the meal typically ends with the dessert course, but there was no concept of dessert in the Japanese meal before the introduction of Western cuisines and eating habits into the Japanese lifestyle. The dessert in a Western meal is usually sweet, using ample amounts of sugar, while the other dishes, including the main dishes or salads, call for very little sugar as a rule. In Japanese dining, on the other hand, sweets were not traditionally served at the end of the meal, but sugar was used in some of the main-course dishes. Sukiyaki, a tabletop dish of beef and vegetables, for example, would be tasteless without sugar. Japanese also eat various beans at dinner, and most of them are cooked with sugar.

Some of the foreign students in my classes say that the sugar we have in Japan is slightly different from the varieties they are used to at home. Sugar beets are grown in the northern island of Hokkaido and sugar cane grows on southern islands like Okinawa, but domestic producers can satisfy only about 30% of domestic consumption needs. The remaining 70% is met by imports of crude sugar from other countries. The crude sugar is locally processed and refined to satisfy Japanese tastes and needs. Thus, slight differences in taste may come from the refining process and the need to please distinctive local demands.

Most sugar in Japan does not contain molasses. Molasses is usually eliminated at an early stage in the refining process. There are even light brown-colored sugars without molasses, which some people seem to find confusing. The color of the sugar actually depends on its degree of refinement. The more purified the sugar, the whiter—and less sweet—it becomes.

There are some well-known sugars in Japan, however, that *do* contain molasses. The best-known variety is called *kuro-zato* (literally "dark colored sugar") and is produced in Kagoshima, in southwestern Kyushu, the main southern island. This sugar comes in crude but fragile rocks that are originally fairly large but are usually broken into fist-sized or smaller lumps. Brown sugar containing molasses is now widely available, but is primarily used in baking cakes and cookies, a sign of the influence of Western cooking. Another sugar containing molasses which is best known by professionals in the food business is the fine, powdery white sugar called *wasanbon*. This expensive sugar is so fine it melts immediately in your mouth. Because of its delicate and elegant flavor, and the ease with which it can be molded, *wasanbon* is used to make traditional local sweets which are served with tea.

For daily cooking, select the type of sugar based on the purpose of its use. For the ordinary purpose of sweetening a dish, regular white sugar should be fine. If you are cooking something slowly over low heat so that it is well-seasoned inside and out, like some fish or beans, you may prefer sugar in large crystals (*zaramé*), as it will dissolve more slowly than smaller granules of sugar, and it will nicely permeate the inside of the food being cooked. Brown sugar without molasses may also be preferred as a sweetener in slow cooking because it is sweeter than refined white sugar, but it will not give you the unique aroma of molasses that many cooks prefer.

In this book, unless otherwise specified, you can cook with regular white sugar. You may find that Japanese white sugar tastes slightly different from your native varieties of sugar, but the difference will prove negligible to the overall taste of the dish.

Liquid Candy (*Mizu-amé*)
Mizu-amé is a sweet, sticky liquid, similar to corn syrup, which is traditionally made from glutinous rice. Today, however, *mizu-amé* may be made from starches from other sources. It is used as a sweetener in traditional sweet toppings for desserts.

SWEET COOKING RICE WINE (*Mirin*)

Unlike regular rice wine (*saké*), which is made from regular short-grain Japanese rice, sweet cooking rice wine, or *mirin*, is made from a glutinous rice called *mochi-gomé*. This glutinous rice is also used to make rice cakes, or *mochi*. Rice malt (*koji*) and an indigenous liquor distilled from grains or sweet potatoes (*shochu*) are also used to make *mirin*.

Mirin, which contains about 13.5% alcohol, is a thick yellow wine that tastes quite sweet. It is solely for cooking, not for drinking. It gives the food a very light, sweet taste, and its good flavor helps counteract any unpleasant smells from the other ingredients. It also adds luster to the food, so it is a frequent addition to sauces for basting fish or chicken before grilling, to ensure a beautiful glaze.

You can buy *mirin* at a liquor store or a grocery or supermarket that has a liquor license. At other grocery stores and supermarkets, you will often find a product called *shin-mirin* ("new sweet cooking rice wine) or *mirin-fumi* (*mirin*-like taste) that is sold as a substitute for *mirin*, similar to the "cooking rice wine" that is marketed instead of real saké. Although sweet and thick like *mirin*, these *mirin* substitutes contain less alcohol and do not seem to work in quite the same way as *mirin* in the cooking process. You may wish to try *shin-mirin* yourself and see the difference.

VINEGAR (*Su*)

Rice Vinegar (*Kome-zu*)
What you will find at a Japanese food store under the name "vinegar" is mainly vinegar made from rice (*su* or *zu*). However, the rice vinegar which is brewed by the traditional method using polished rice is more specifically called *komé-zu* or *yoné-zu*.

The acidity of rice vinegar is about 4.5%, which is less than that of American bottled cider vinegar, which is diluted with water for pickling and for table use. *Su* is also milder than American white vinegar, and many foreign residents prefer it. I have recommended to my students that rice vinegar, or *komé-zu*, should be used not only in Japanese cooking but for Western dishes as well, for pickling or even salad dressing. My husband, who likes sour dishes, sometimes nearly chokes when he eats something flavored with a strongly acidic vinegar, but this reaction is much less likely with *komé-zu*.

Rice vinegar adds more than sour flavor to food. It has a unique mild taste, produced by the 70-some different acids and amino acids used in the brewing process. It minimizes salty tastes, prevents discoloration of some foods and preserves them longer. But *komé-zu* is most frequently used to season sauces and in dressings for some Japanese salads.

Other Types of Vinegar

Kuro-zu: This vinegar is nearly black in color, a result of its long fermentation. Although it is basically brewed in the same method as *komé-su*, it is fermented for 1 to 3 years, which causes its color to change. Its distinctive flavor makes it a popular ingredient among many health-conscious consumers, but this vinegar is not suitable for cooking.

Genmai-zu: This vinegar is made from unpolished brown rice, or *genmai*. *Genmai-zu* is quite popular among those concerned about their health but this, too, is not a cooking vinegar.

Kokumotsu-zu: If you find a slightly less expensive Japanese vinegar than the above varieties, it is likely to be *kokumotsu-zu*, which is made from other grains than rice, such as wheat or corn. *Kokumotsu-zu* is suitable for use in cooking, but it lacks the distinctive mild flavor of rice vinegar.

Gosei-zu: I seldom see this vinegar in stores these days, as this synthetic product seems to have fallen out of favor with Japanese, who now prefer natural ingredients for their cooking. *Gosei-zu* is a blend of chemically synthesized acetic acid and seasoning agents.

Fruit vinegar

Fruit vinegars are not used in Japanese cooking, and there are practically no locally brewed products to be found. Those you may find in Japanese stores are probably imported vinegars for use in Western cooking.

Vinegar, in combination with other ingredients, is used to make a great variety of dressings. I have introduced various distinctive dressings in the recipes that call for them.

You should always store vinegar in a dark, cool place, but the best way to ensure that you are always using fresh vinegar is to buy the smallest bottle of vinegar available.

FATS AND OILS (*Abura*)

Until the mid-19th century, most Japanese did not eat animal meat. They abstained from slaughtering animals for food due to the influence of Buddhism, which was introduced to Japan many centuries ago. They neither raised animals for their meat nor commonly raised dairy cattle. Not surprisingly, vegetable oils were more commonly used in cooking than animal fats in the past.

Among the various vegetable oils used by the Japanese in cooking, sesame oil seems to have the longest history. Today, with the growing popularity of such Western dishes as salads, demand for vegetable oils has increased, and consumption of sesame oil has been outpaced by that of oil produced from soybeans, rapeseed, cottonseeds and corn. The use of oils thought to be good for one's health, such as safflower oil, is also increasing among health-conscious Japanese.

A favorite Japanese dish is deep-fried vegetable and seafood tempura. Tempura dishes have a crispy bite, and the deep-frying allows the fresh vegetables and seafood to retain their original textures and flavors. The ideal oil to use for deep-frying will remain stable at high levels of heat for long periods and will not easily become oxidized. It should not smoke when frying foods or result in much discoloration of the ingredients.

Many oils sold in stores today are labeled "salad oil," and according to their labels they are suitable for both deep-frying and for use in salad dressings. However, consumers can also purchase a type of oil called "tempura oil," which is specifically formulated for tempura frying. This oil often includes sesame oil, which helps turns fried foods crisp and an appetizing golden brown color. Cooks could use sesame oil by itself for deep-frying, but it has a rather strong flavor of its own—a familiar taste in Chinese cooking—which some people dislike. This type of sesame oil is made from roasted sesame seeds which are dark in color and which give the oil its distinctive flavor. A better choice for deep-frying is a light-colored sesame oil which has very little flavor of its own.

Oils are blended to allow cooks to use them for multiple purposes, such as for frying and for salad dressings. Single-source oils are named for their source, e.g. sesame oil, safflower oil, or cottonseed oil, but such products as salad oil or tempura oil are typically blended oils.

FLOURS AND STARCHES
(*Kona* or *Ko*)

Flours made from different grains may look alike, but they behave surprisingly differently when they are cooked. In my years of teaching cooking, I have often been asked about flours or received troubled calls from students when flours haven't performed as expected.

In Japan we have flours made from a variety of grains, some of which I use everyday and others that I seldom employ. I have found that Americans or other foreign residents unfamiliar with Japanese flours often have problems when they first try to bake a cake, so in this section I will explain about common flours found at the grocery store and how they are typically used.

Cornstarch (*Kon sutachi*)
Cornstarch, which was introduced here from the West, is called *kon sutachi* in Japanese as well. It is usually sold in small plastic bags printed with a design featuring cobs of corn. It is used in cooking the same way that cornstarch is used in the West.

Glutinous Rice Flour (*Shiratama-ko*, *mochiko*, sweet rice flour)
This flour is made from a sweet, glutinous rice or a 50-50 mixture of glutinous rice and regular Japanese rice. The rice is milled and soaked in cold water for blending purposes, in the form of paste or dough. Then it is sun-dried to produce solid lumps, and the lumps are broken apart into fine pieces and packed in small bags. The flour is used in Japanese pastries eaten as snacks or desserts, including *shiratama*, which literally means "white balls." *Shiratama-ko* is typically combined with water, kneaded and formed into small white balls. The balls are boiled in water, and served with sweetened adzuki beans.

Potato Starch (*Katakuri-ko*)
This is the most common thickening agent in Japanese cooking. The Japanese word *katakuri-ko* actually refers to a starch which is obtained from the root of a wild lily called *katakuri*, and which used to be the major thickening agent used in Japan. However, because the available supply could not satisfy the demand, potato starch became more popular and both became known by the same name. It now seems nearly impossible to find genuine *katakuri-ko*.

As a thickening agent, especially for soups and sauces, I find potato starch to be much more effective than cornstarch. It has a mild effect and can easily be controlled to produce the desired consistency. In my classes, however, I am often asked whether cornstarch can substitute for potato starch in cooking. It can, but I always recommend that the amount of cornstarch used should be only half of the amount of potato starch, because cornstarch has a much stronger effect. The difference is not just thickness. Soups or sauces cooked with cornstarch thicken when they cool, but dishes containing potato starch retain the same thickness and consistency. You must take care, though, to cook dishes containing potato starch thoroughly, because if the dish is not cooked well, the potato starch will separate again from the water when it cools. When using potato starch as a thickener, be sure to cook the dish for an extra minute after boiling to ensure it's completely cooked.

Originally, the genuine *katakuri-ko* was also used to make a kind of soft pap for those who were ill and lacked any appetite. The *katakuri-ko* was combined with hot water and stirred to make a paste, then sweetened with sugar. I liked the dish as a child, but have never tried it since.

Rice Flour (*Joshin-ko*)
The ordinary rice which the Japanese eat as a staple food is milled to make this flour. It is usually used for Japanese pastries. We do not add yeast soda or baking powder to rice flour and glutinous rice flour to make them rise, as we do with wheat flour. Instead, rice flour is kneaded with hot water, pounded, and then steamed. These traditional steamed pastries come in a wide variety of shapes and colors, although most of them feature a filling of sweet bean paste.

Roasted Soybean Flour (*Kina-ko*)
Soybeans are roasted and ground into powder to make this light yellow flour. It is typically used as a topping for various pastries, due to its distinctive flavor and color and a taste that stimulates the appetite.

These pastries are now mainly made by confectioners, and the flour is rarely used in home cooking. But when Japanese prepare rice cakes, or *mochi*, they often use *kina-ko* to top the freshly pounded *mochi*, as well as sweet red beans. At home, when my parents and in-laws were visiting, I used to make small rice balls with steamed glutinous rice and coat them with a mixture of *kina-ko* and sugar on days marking the spring and autumn equinox, when we held a small memorial service for our ancestors. When I was a child, I often ate *kina-ko* mixed with sugar, as I liked its roasted flavor.

Kina-ko is sold in a small plastic bag with the name *kina-ko* on it.

Tempura Flour (*Tempura-ko*)

A good batter is essential to making tasty tempura. The batter depends on several factors, including the type of flour used, the temperature of the water that is added, the way they are mixed, and the proportions of flour and water. Using tempura flour will allay many of your concerns, helping you to produce perfect batter every time, no matter how good a cook you are.

Tempura-ko is a special flour strictly intended for use in making tempura. It contains wheat flour, wheat starch, powdered egg yolks, baking powder, salt, amino acids, carotene and other ingredients that make tempura look and taste good. It is usually sold in paper bags half the size of bags of regular wheat flour, and labeled with the name *tempura-ko*.

To use tempura flour, mix 1 cup of the flour lightly with $3/4$ cup cold water. You need not mix the batter until smooth.

Wheat Flour (*Komugi-ko, meriken-ko*)

Newly arrived foreign residents in my cooking classes often ask me about the wheat flour in Japan. They note that the flour they buy here behaves differently in baking than the flour at home, and ask the differences between the different varieties that are sold. Americans ask where they can buy all-purpose flour, while the British often ask if self-rising flour is available.

Because of this interest, I did quite a bit of research on this topic, even visiting the laboratory of a large flour mill to learn more about the flours produced in Japan. I now tell my cooking students as well as students in my shopping classes all about wheat flour here. This is what I tell them:

Japan no longer grows much wheat, so most of the wheat here is imported, mainly from North America. There are two types of imported wheats, a hard wheat grain and a soft wheat grain. The difference between the two is the amount of gluten each contains.

The hard wheat grain contains about 13% gluten, and flour milled from this grain is for making yeast breads and other dough which uses yeast, such as pizza dough. This flour is called *kyoryoku-ko*, which literally means "powerful flour." It is sold in a package that features a design of bread rolls.

The soft wheat grain is milled into two types of flour: one containing 7-8% gluten made of the inner part of the grain, and one made from the outer part of the grain and containing 9–10% gluten. The flour with 7–8% gluten is used to make tempura batter and for soft cakes like chiffon cakes. Many of my American students, however, complain that cakes made with this flour are too soft. The flour is sold in a package featuring a design of small violet flowers. The flour is called *hakuriki-ko*, which literally means "weak flour," as it is actually less elastic (or powerful) than *kyoryoku-ko*. The flour with 9–10% gluten is used for general cooking and baking, and it is the most popular flour on the market. It is sold in a package featuring orange margaret flowers or with a red heart design. This is also known as a "weak flour," or *hakuriki-ko*.

All-purpose or self-rising flours are not available in Japan. To get a flour which resembles these flours, however, I recommend mixing *kyoryoku-ko* (strong flour) and *hakuriki-ko* (weak flour) at a proportion of 7 to 3. Even a 50-50 mixture of these two types of flour will produce something fairly close to all-purpose flour. For self-rising flour, use this flour and add a suitable amount of baking powder.

You can also purchase a flour made of local wheat. It contains 11–12% gluten, a ratio in between the two other main varieties, so it is called *churiki-ko*, or medium strength flour. Although the gluten content resembles that of all-purpose or self-rising flour, this flour is not suitable for baking bread or other baked goods. It is used to make traditional white noodles like *udon* and *somen*.

INDEX